THE GRAND TOURS OF
KATHERINE WILMOT

THE GRAND TOURS OF
KATHERINE WILMOT

France 1801–3 and
Russia 1805–7

─────

COMPILED AND EDITED BY
ELIZABETH MAVOR

WEIDENFELD AND NICOLSON
LONDON

First published in Great Britain in 1992
by George Weidenfeld and
Nicolson Limited
91 Clapham High Street
London SW4 7TA

British Library Cataloguing in
Publication Date is available

ISBN 0 297 81223 8

Photoset by Deltatype Ltd,
Ellesmere Port, Cheshire
Printed in Great Britain by
Butler & Tanner Ltd
Frome and London

Contents

For Robin Whitworth and Tony King-Harman

Acknowledgements

I should like to thank the Royal Irish Academy for permission to use the transcripts of Katherine Wilmot's Russian journals in their possession, and I should particularly like to thank their librarian, Mrs Brigid Dolan, for much kind and patient help.

I am also most grateful to Colonel A. L. King-Harman OBE DL for permission to use his transcript of Katherine Wilmot's Continental tour with his ancestress, Lady Mount Cashell, as I am for his kind loan of rare books. For this I must also thank Mr H. Boggis-Rolfe CB CBE.

I should also like to thank Miss Janet Adam for generous permission to reproduce the portrait of her great, great, great grand-aunt, Katherine Wilmot.

It remains to thank Mrs Sybil Cook for her excellent typing, and Rosemary Legge at Weidenfeld for her careful preparation of the manuscript for publication.

Introduction

The journals of Katherine Wilmot celebrate not one, but two Grand Tours – to the European Continent from 1801–3, and to Russia from 1805–7. The intervening years appear to have been spent at the family home at Glanmire, near Cork, 'in my Gazebo', as Katherine appealingly puts it, 'where, bending like a willow over Shandon Steeple my days, leaf by leaf, will drop into the Tomb . . .'[1]

Such elegiac musing belied the enthusiasm with which this young Irish gentlewoman set out on her travels, and the dash and sparkle with which she recorded them.

The background to the first tour was that temporary lull in hostilities between France and Great Britain which was marked by the Peace of Amiens in 1802. For ten revolutionary years the charms of the Continent had been denied the English. Now, though the necessary sea voyage had to be faced, a prospect compensatingly alluring welcomed the brave traveller on the other side.

Waiting was Paris, with Napoleon as First Consul, now at 'the very peak and weathercock of greatness'.[2] Available once again were the delights of Parisian society, its theatres, its opera houses. Flung open to all (since they were now state owned) were the National monuments: the Tuileries, the Palais Royal, the Invalides, not to mention pleasure parks, museums and galleries, the last crammed with pillaged works of art from Napoleon's campaigns in Italy.

For those educated in horror by the popular Gothic novels of the time sterner pleasures were at hand; the nailed-up door of the poor dead Queen's bedroom, still bearing the marks of the mob that had beaten it down on the terrible night of 6 October 1789; the Place de la Concorde, site of the Guillotine, where, when it rained, aristocratically purple blood was said to ooze interestingly from beneath the paving stones.

All this and more lay ahead in late November 1801 as Katherine Wilmot and her travelling companions, Lord and Lady Mount Cashell, waited in London for their French passports.

Katherine had already armed herself with a new journal, inscribing on its fly-leaf that she would 'every now and then record the events of the day', adding quaintly, 'so that like a snail, wherever I crawl I may be known for the trail which I shall leave smeared behind me in the book . . .'[3]

From then on the events of the day were indeed faithfully recorded. Her method, judging from the only personal journal which remains (from 26 October 1806 – 23 October 1807), was each Monday to record retrospectively the events of the previous week. These were then worked up into a sequence of bulletins, and dispatched to her elder brother, Robert, back in Ireland. The choice of recipient was significant, for her brother was to influence both style and subject matter of her writing.

Asides in his sister's journal give some idea, if only negatively, of the preferences of this humorous and intelligent lawyer:

'. . . people, I believe interest you more than places . . .'[4]

'I don't want to tease you by admiring what I know you abhor . . .'[5] [Republican sentiments]

'. . . an exhibition of Modern Painters, which, (don't be frightened) I am not going to describe . . .'[6]
and affectionately:

'Wiseacre that you are!'[7]

This dominie-like presence hovering off-page had a certain restricting effect. An examination of her one remaining personal journal reveals that Katherine suppressed in bulletins home, her own nervous headaches, wheezing attacks, anxiety and occasional boredom.

Having said this, the journal she sent her brother was remarkably uninhibited, though in this she was not extra-ordinary, for it was an uninhibited age, and a good age therefore in which to keep a journal. Botany, scenery, customs, architec-ture (though sparingly), fashion, food, sexual mores, bed bugs, the upbringing of children, moderate scandal, all feature in her writing, so that from the moment she and Lady Mount Cashell drive into Paris with their eyes 'flying out of their sockets' both Robert and we know ourselves to be in for a round of vicarious fun.

For she was not only well educated, familiar with the literature of her own country, that of Germany, Italy and France, as well as the classics (if only in translation), she was curious and broad-minded, interested in people of both high and low degree. Unlike Maria Edgeworth and Fanny Burney, who were also busy keeping journals of life in post-Revolutionary Paris, Katherine was not censorious. Going in at the top end of society with the Mount Cashells, she was not alarmed to mix with what Maria Edgeworth considered the contaminating *nouveaux riches* of the new order, nor yet with Republican circles (Lady Mount Cashell was an enthusiastic Republican in any case). She moved serenely round High Society noting its quiddities and peccadil-loes with an amused eye, and with much irreverent enjoyment.

In Italy, where if possible she enjoyed herself even more, high spots in the journal were to include exciting brushes with *banditti*, and a tense but thrilling passage in 1803 when as a consequence of Napoleon resuming the war with Great Britain, she was for a time bottled up in Florence.

'Ransoms were speculated upon,' she writes of the unhappy English tourists, 'chains and dungeons glanced at, Gentlemen went off in disguise at the peril of their lives – ladies fainted!'[8]

Robert proved an excellent taskmaster. By the time his sister had returned from the Continent and was setting out for Russia to bring home their younger sister who was on a visit there, she had found her true 'voice', vivacious, witty, sensitive, as well as analytic. It is a voice that puts one a little in mind perhaps of Jane

Austen's Elizabeth Bennet. It is also a compassionate voice, and one sufficiently 'romantic' to capture the exotic Russian scene.

She was to dine *alfresco* with three wild Georgian princes: 'I caught a glimpse of their mustachos and bare throats, scarfs, and diamond rings through the spreading branches of fruit trees which shaded all the table with the most refreshing green.'[9]

It is a moment, a Russian moment, and perfectly seen. This is important, for the Russia Katherine Wilmot evokes for us is the Russia of Tolstoy's *War and Peace*.

This time her journals were written for a sister-in-law and two younger sisters, and for them she re-created high life as it was being lived in the aristocratic Russian houses of the day. It so happened that her maid, Eleanor Cavanagh, perhaps in emulation of her mistress, was also writing her version of events for the entertainment of her old father back at Glanmire. As in some Mozart opera, mistress and maid in sparkling duet faithfully render events both above and below stairs in the household of their great hostess, the Princess Dashkov.

As a young woman the Princess had played a significant part in the palace revolution which had overthrown the Czar Peter III in favour of his wife, Catherine. Now over sixty, she lived in semi-retirement on her country estate south of Moscow where Matty, Katherine's younger sister, was currently installed as a much-loved guest.

Katherine's portrait of this extraordinary woman, whose influence was to open wide the doors of Russian society to the two Wilmot sisters, is wonderfully telling:

'I wish you were to see the Princess go out to take a walk, or rather to look over her subjects! An old brown greatcoat and a silk handkerchief about her neck, worn to rags is her dress, and well may it be worn to rags for she has worn it 18 years . . . she helps the masons to build walls, she assists with her own hands in making the roads, she feeds the cows, she composes music, she sings and plays, she writes for the press, she shells the corn, she talks out loud in the Church and corrects the Priest if he is not devout, she talks out loud in her little theatre and puts in the

xiv

performers when they are out in their parts, she is doctor, and apothecary, a surgeon, a farrier, a carpenter, a magistrate, a lawyer. . . .'[10]

Katherine and her maid arrived in Russia at about the time the Czar Alexander had signed a treaty with Great Britain against Napoleon. They left in 1807 two months after he had signed another with Napoleon against Great Britain. Indeed on the homeward voyage their ship only just escaped being caught up in the English bombardment of Copenhagen. To Katherine this was something of a disappointment, she had wanted to see the fun.

Had she lived longer, she would certainly have travelled again, evoking other scenes and other lives, for the delight of her friends and herself. The Levant had long attracted her, the East might have beckoned, and she would then surely and deservedly have joined the ranks of the Mary Wortley Montagus, the Hester Stanhopes. This sadly did not happen. As it was, though other women like Fanny Burney, Maria Edgeworth and Miss Berry wrote as amusingly as herself on post-Revolutionary Paris, no other English traveller of the period has surpassed her vivid and intelligent study of Russia as it was before the invasion of Napoleon. In particular should she be remembered for her unique and sympathetic observations of the Russian peasant culture which she saw at first hand on the Princess Dashkov's estate at Troitskoe and in which she found much resembling that of the Irish.

Though friends had urged their publication as early as 1812, her journals were ignored after her death in 1824. It was not until the early years of the present century that transcripts of the journals were discovered and lodged in the library of the Royal Irish Academy in Dublin.

In 1920, almost a hundred years after her death, her Continental journal edited by Thomas U. Sadleir was published under the title of *An Irish Peer on the Continent*. Her Russian journal edited by Lady Londonderry and H. M. Hyde followed in 1934, as *The Russian Journals and Letters of Martha and Catherine Wilmot*.

The present book aims at giving the reader as wide a selection as possible from Katherine's writings, but although it comprises only about a third of the total corpus of her writing, it includes hitherto unpublished material, and this has been indicated in the Notes.

I have retained Katherine's original spelling, which for some curious reason Lady Londonderry chose to render more archaic than it actually is, substituting 'sais' for 'says', 'eneough' for 'enough', and inventing abbreviations which Katherine did not always use. In the interests of the modern reader I have broken up some of Katherine's longer paragraphs, smoothed out certain complexities of punctuation, and curtailed her unrestricted use of the capitals which can alas no longer enlarge our understanding of the text.

I hope that in doing so I have not taken anything away, but rather brought out the colloquial vigour of her writing, that delightful and intelligent exuberance which is so very much her own.

1

Travelling Companions

The party set out from Ireland for London in September 1801, Lord and Lady Mount Cashell, their friend, Katherine Wilmot, their daughters, Helena and Jane, and four servants. It was a young party, the Mount Cashells barely into their thirties, and Katherine only two years younger.

A three-month tour of England had originally been planned, but the news that peace preliminaries were now taking place between England and France had encouraged the friends to extend their visit by a trip to the Continent.

Anticipations no doubt ran high, though these must have been considerably diminished by the existing tension between the Earl and his Countess. Lady Mount Cashell who had married her husband when she had been nineteen and he twenty-one had originally seen him as 'a handsome man', which a portrait confirms, 'with gentle manners and the appearance of an easy temper.'[1]

Ten years had gone by since then, however, and Lady Mount Cashell with leisure to reflect had come to perceive certain flaws in the Earl. Her husband's education, she now realized 'had been of the meanest sort', his understanding 'uncultivated and his mind contracted.'[2] Worse still, from her own highly cultivated point of view, he exhibited a positive aversion to literature, was incapable of comprehending the feelings of a noble spirit [her own], and worst of all for one of her avowedly radical sympathies, respected nothing but wealth and titles.

How fair this assessment was is hard to tell. Lord Mount Cashell seems not to have been interested in politics (unlike his

1

wife), to have preferred living on his country estate to staying in town, and to have been a just and 'improving' landlord. He appears further to have been amiable, though otherwise nothing out of the ordinary, for when the British Minister Plenipotentiary entertained the Mount Cashells in Paris, it was the Earl's wife and her friend, Miss Wilmot, who were particularly noticed, the Earl was not mentioned.

'How he came to think of me for a wife God alone knows,' mournfully commented Lady Mount Cashell, 'a man whose character was perfectly opposite to mine.'[3]

She was the second of the twelve children of Lord Kingsborough later Earl of Kingston, whose family in the reign of Queen Elizabeth had migrated to Ireland from Feathercock Hall near Northallerton in Yorkshire. When she was fourteen her mother, Lady Kingsborough, had made the cardinal error of employing as her governess, the young radical intellectual, Mary Wollstonecraft, who had been recommended by the Undermaster at Eton.

At the time Mary had already written, though not published, her revolutionary *Thoughts on the Education of Daughters*. Had she done so poor Lady Kingsborough might have acted rather differently. As it was her impressionable daughter fell promptly and for ever under the influence of her new governess. In the fullness of time Margaret blossomed out as a Republican, a Freethinker, and a friend of those of the most extravagant political sympathies. She was, however, also a woman of charm and presence.

In appearance Margaret Mount Cashell was large, and according to William Godwin, whom the erstwhile governess of the Countess had married, 'uncommonly tall and brawny with bad teeth, white eyes, and a handsome countenance. She commonly dresses, as I have seen Mrs Fenwick dressed out of poverty, with a grey gown, and no linen visible; but with gigantic arms, which she commonly folds, naked and exposed almost up to the shoulders.'[4]

There is certainly an element of exaggeration, even malice in

2

the description, though it points to an androgynous quality in Lady Mount Cashell which might have caused her to be drawn both to Mary Wollstonecraft and to Katherine Wilmot. Certainly Lady Mount Cashell's height, and Katherine Wilmot's petite figure later encouraged them to attend a masquerade together in Paris, Lady Mount Cashell as a cavalier, Miss Wilmot as her *inamorata*.

It is unsurprising that such a woman should have differed from her husband in almost everything, from the education of their children to opinions on politics, and these differences had become increasingly marked up to the time of setting out on their European tour.

To the exasperation of the Earl, Margaret Mount Cashell had supported Wolfe Tone's Society of United Irishmen, an organization founded on Republican principles and dedicated to ousting the English from Ireland with the help of Revolutionary France. She had also supported the subsequent unsuccessful revolution of 1798, and mutinously opposed the Act of Union with England which followed in 1800.

Perhaps it was to the credit of both parties that they should, in the interests of domestic tranquillity, have invited Katherine Wilmot to be of their party on their Continental adventure.

Fortunately Katherine had recently been left a legacy by a grandmother, a sum happily too substantial to be spent on trifles, it seems, 'too small to be laid by as a fortune'.[5] What better use for it than travel.

Katherine would prove an excellent choice. Her family home at Glanmire was not far from the Mount Cashells' at Moore Park, near Cork, where she was a frequent visitor. She came from an impeccable background (ultimately going back to ancient Derbyshire stock), was one of an exceptionally happy family of nine children, had a gift for friendship, and was witty, broad minded and well educated, the last appealing particularly to Margaret Mount Cashell, who was a self-styled intellectual. Katherine, however, seems not to have shared her friend's more extreme views, nor yet her enthusiasm for English Republicans, something that must have endeared her to the conservative-minded Earl.

It must consequently have been in a cheerful and more than usually emollient state of mind that the party prepared for France: '. . . you may fancy Lord and Lady Mount Cashell,' wrote Katherine, 'Helena, Jane and me pack'd in the Family Coach, with Mary Lawless, Mary Smith, Blanchois, and William in another carriage, driving full speed, nine Irish Adventurers, to the French dominions.'[6]

The France towards which they were travelling had for the last ten years been convulsed by change. There existed no longer a King, nor yet an established religion; the calendar had been changed to a Revolutionary one, time itself altered, since the Republican clock was divided into ten rather than twelve hours. But at last the era of Revolutionary wars in which France had continuously fought against the coalitions of the great European powers had for the time drawn to a close.

The welcome awaiting on the other side of the Channel was to astonish some English travellers. 'Is it not very curious,' wrote one, 'that we should meet with such a reception at Boulogne, into which place Nelson a few weeks ago since was pouring death and devastation!'[7]

The same commentator noted with amusement how the French were responding to their capital being overrun by English tourists. 'Boots titivated here on the English gout,'[8] he read pinned up in a window, remarking that the French themselves were everywhere affecting their idea of current English fashion, that is to say, whiskers, cropped hair, unshaven chins, boots.

The sightseers thronging Paris were not confined to the leisured classes it seems, for according to one observer it was barely possible to move without meeting whole families of the English bourgeoisie waddling along like ducks or standing rooted to the spot gawping at the sights. Five guineas all-in ensured them a comfortable passage over, twenty-four hours in Paris with a night at the theatre, and nothing further to spend since the museums and sights of the capital were free.

The general impression gained by unsophisticated travellers on arrival in Paris was of immensely high buildings (so shadowed, the ground-floor inhabitants were forced to light candles at noonday), dirty streets, the 'disquieting sexual differences' all too plainly discernible on the colossal statues, and the displeasing rendezvous of upwards of two hundred courtesans each evening outside the Théâtre des Variétés, which made it a 'recepticle of obscenity'.[9]

More sophisticated visitors discovered with interest that the once obligatory titles of 'Citoyen' and 'Citoyenne' 'are getting quite vulgar, and they will soon be out of fashion with the lowest',[10] the *ci-devant* address of Monsieur and Madame taking their place.

Horace Walpole's friend, Miss Berry, a pre-Revolutionary habituée of Paris, and now approaching middle age, was to confide some interesting observations to her journal.

In her coach on the way up from Calais she noticed the improved state of cultivation in the countryside, that the cottages were better kept, the children better fed. But she saw also a mournful progression of decaying chateaux and neglected churches, though in one village she was pleased to see that the words *'Temple de la Raison'* written up on the church had been recently painted over.

In Paris itself though the boulevards were as gay as she remembered, and the Hôtel d'Orleans 'not one pin altered since I saw it 16 years ago',[11] she was quick to notice the decline in courtesy among the new set, how their clothes were ill cut, like clothes made by a village tailor, how at table the covers were served all at once, and twice as much meat as before consumed in half the time. She also found that old Sèvres, bought for nothing from the great aristocratic houses, was selling at a quarter of its original price, displaced by the fashionable Sèvres 'à l'antique', in what Miss Berry considered ugly, odd, dark colours like tortoiseshell and steel with gold borders.

In spite of certain unfavourable impressions Miss Berry was nonetheless determined to make a careful study of the new

Paris, and by no means to confine herself to the society of *ci-devant* aristos. Of these, as she robustly asserted, there were plenty back home in England, and it was the New Society she was eager to encounter. In this she contrasted with Maria Edgeworth, who had arrived in the capital on a sight-seeing tour with her father. '. . . we hear from all sides that we see only the best of Paris', she wrote in her journal, 'the men of literature and the *ancienne noblesse. Les nouveaux riches* are quite a different set. My father has seen something of them at Madame Tallien's (now Cabarus) and was disgusted.'[12] An opinion, that when Katherine herself met Madame Tallien, was vigorously contradicted.

Madame Tallien was one of the figureheads of the New Society of distinguished men and women English travellers were wild to meet. It included people like Lafayette, Talleyrand, Chateaubriand, Talma, Vestris and the painter David round whom, according to one visitor 'Humanity has drawn a sable circle.'[13] This since the painter had been a friend of Robespierre, had frequently sketched the victims of the guillotine, and had been heard to say the heads of 20,000 more must roll before 'the great work of philosophy could be accomplished'.[14] One visitor had been thrilled to glimpse him in his garden 'wearing a dirty robe and an old hat'[15] much as Miss Berry herself had encountered the famous authoress and salon hostess, Germaine de Staël, 'in an excessively dirty cabinet – sofa singularly so,'[16] wearing an old spencer. Though more approvingly she also met Madame Recamier, '*the* decided beauty of the *new world*'.[17]

More than anyone else, however, people wanted to meet the First Consul himself, and if this were not possible, his wife, or at least his mother.

This, however, was not always easy. 'I have heard much of the visit of Mrs Damer and Miss Berry to Paris, and their difficulty to get introduced to the first Consul,' wrote Fanny Burney, going on to report Miss Berry as complaining, 'We have been everywhere – seen everything, heard everybody – beheld such sights! listened to such discourse! joined such society! and all to obtain his [Napoleon's] notice – and all in vain!'[18]

6

Miss Berry was ultimately to achieve her objective, though Mrs Damer, her friend, was less successful. (She had brought over one of her own works, a sculpture of the radical politician, Charles James Fox, to present to Napoleon.)

By enlisting the help of an enterprising Swiss tailor, Miss Berry managed not only to penetrate to Madame Bonaparte's apartment (all in blue-lilac lutestring embroidered in honey-suckle) but to hers and the First Consul's bedchamber 'the one where they actually both sleep in one bed,'[19] as Miss Berry expressed it. This apartment, done out in blue silk with white and gold fringes, the bed of solid mahogany, greatly surpassed the magnificence of both Versailles and the Petit Trianon in the old days, or so Miss Berry claimed.

For Katherine Wilmot and the Mount Cashells, however, there was to be no necessity of employing the services of enterprising Swiss tailors. From the first moment of their setting foot in France, all doors were open to them.

2

Continental Journal

The 29th Novr. [1801] at 3 o'clock in the morning, we got on board the *Countess of Elgin*, commanded by Captain Sampson, and Lady Mount Cashell smuggled in her suite Monsieur Amoulin a young Frenchman who couldn't get a passport. But that unfortunately he was a stupid, clumsy piece of goods, we should have been amus'd at the mystery that attended the transaction.

After a desperately rough passage of five hours, and a cruel delay before we were permitted to land, occasion'd by our names being written down and reported to the municipality, we at length got on shore, reeling after our sufferings, and in that plight, we were taken to the custom house, transferr'd from thence to the municipal officers, and then to the examination of the commissaires.

They were the most shocking sharks I ever saw altogether. Even after trunks, pocket books, writing cases, green baize bags, etc., were quietly deliver'd in, they put their hands into our pockets and then felt down our sides, even to our ankles, for contraband commodities.

At length we were walk'd up by our national guard to the Hotel Dessein and were soon put into good humour, by the contemplation of novelty, which struck our senses in every direction and such a quick hocus pocus metamorphosis from what we had left in England a few hours before.

8

Every man in a cock'd hat, three colour'd cockade and gold ear-rings, savage black whiskers and frequently a muff on his arm. Indeed this was the costume of every ragged poltroon. The grisettes, pretty and smartly adorn'd with sparkling crosses, necklaces, ear-rings and every shining decoration, with close caps upon their round rosy cheeks, and an air of courtesy and ease, which controll'd the intrusive part of that curiosity, which obviously our foreign appearance inspired. Their cheerful style of manners did not strike me either with any of the servility that preceded the Revolution, or the brusque effect of recent emancipation. . . .

I scarcely know how I spent the first day, what with the effects of illness, and the sight of so many incongruities! This much I remember, that we sat down to a most splendid repast, not a single dish of which I had ever seen before, and during the dinner (the successive courses of which I thought would never end) we were symphoniz'd by Republican tunes, play'd outside the window, on the organ and tambourines, and a hundred compliments passed on the arrival of a *Mi Lor Anglois*.

Monday 30th Novr. [1801]
On waking at a very early hour with the confusion incident to that state, you will laugh at me when I confess to you the flash of transport I experienced in saying to myself 'I absolutely then am in France,' and in drawing aside the curtain of my bed to prove it to myself, by contemplating the painted ceiling, the white marble tables, the looking-glass panels, the polish'd oak floor, and all the little circumstances of difference in the apartment.

Without exception I never remember in all my life a moment of such unfeign'd extacy! Instinctively I fancied some metamorphoses was taking place in me, and putting up my hand, to try if my nightcap at least was not turning into a 'cap of Liberty' (still leaning out of bed), I lost my balance and down I flump'd upon the floor, to the utter destruction of all my glorious visions and abhorring those prodigious looking glasses, which

9

multiplied my downfall without mercy, in every direction and wherever I turned my eyes.

Getting into bed again in due humiliation I hid my head under the cloaths, ruminating on my disgrace when the door open'd and Lady Mount Cashell, in her white dressing gown appear'd before my eyes. She neither, cou'd compose her senses to rest, so animated were they by the cause which had been so fatal to me, and therefore fully countenancing one another in every sanguine anticipation of pleasure, we agreed to sally forth in quest of adventures. . . .

. . . maybe the best plan will be for me to observe a profound silence on every circumstance touching Calais, since truth compels me to confess that I was in a kind of delirium during the entire time I stay'd in that place, ugly as the town is and deplorable as was the drenching weather!

Tuesday the 1st Decr. [1801]
We quitted Calais in the most deplorable day of storm and rain, that ever came out of the heavens. We pas't through Boulogne, and slept at a little inn at Cormont, as the night was too dangerous, and the roads too bad, to proceed any further. All the country was a dead flat without inclosures and scarcely a tree to be seen. . . .

The 2nd of Decr. [1801]
We passed through Montreuil sur Mer, a fortified town, but mouldering looking like Boulogne – the country pretty much the same. We got into Abbeville to a late dinner, and slept in crimson cloth canopies, the manufacture of the town. Here our friend Mr Amoulin went to join his family, who live near Abbeville and they, being warned of our approach, had invited all the country to a grand ball, for the next week, and did everything they cou'd to make us stay. But we were obliged to proceed.

The 3rd Decr. [1801]

In travelling on, tho' the roads were bad, the country became prettier, with a good many woods. After passing through two or three strongly fortified towns, we got in at three o'clock to Amiens, which is encircled with beautiful grounds.

Two days before Lord Cornwallis* returned from Paris. A Congress for the definitive treaty of Peace is about to be held here. While Lord Mount Cashell went out to see Lord Cornwallis, Lady Mount Cashell and I trotted off, to visit the famous cathedral, which is reckoned the finest and most beautiful in France.

I was surpris'd to find it, so little injur'd, when those in every town we pass'd through before, lay in dreary mouldering desolation about the streets with scarcely two stones together. Many of the convents too exhibited the same deplorable appearance. I don't think I ever saw so fine a building as this Gothic cathedral! By resigning all its silver and riches, at the time of the Revolution, the people of Amiens contrived to preserve it almost entirely uninjured. For the first time I saw canoniz'd noses and fingers, holy relics, the original head of John the Baptist, etc. . . . But to return to the auberge – we had hardly sat down to our dinner, or rather supper, when loud applauses of *Vive la Nation! Vive Bonaparte!* struck our ears and on flying to the window, we saw Joseph Bonaparte† drive by amongst the plaudits of multitudes, who ran at his carriage wheels, welcoming, and proclaiming, at the pitch of their voices, his arrival at Amiens. . . .

4th Decr. [1801]

We left Amiens, pass'd through several vineyards and much cultivated country, fortified towns (which always give the idea of *Much Ado About Nothing*) and dined and slept at Beauvais. . . .

---

* Charles, 1st Marquess Cornwallis (1738–1805), British Ambassador to France.

† Joseph Bonaparte (1768–1844) elder brother of Napoleon and briefly King of Naples and Spain.

Sat. 5th Decr. [1801]

At four o'clock, we drove into Paris with our eyes flying out of their sockets at everything we beheld. The streets struck me as being very narrow and the houses, some of them seven stories high, extremely handsome, and built of stone. *Liberté, Egalité, Fraternité, Propriété Nationale, et Indivisibilité* were written in great letters on all the publick buildings. After stopping at two or three Hotels, at length we found accommodation at *l'Hôtel de l'Europe, Rue de la Loi.*

It is a magnificent house, formerly belonging to some unfortunate *cidevant** noble, the apartments hung throughout with damask and pannel'd with looking glasses of immense size.

Three men attended me up to my bedchamber, to my utter consternation there were none other but themselves to act the part of chamber maids. One had been a soldier, and had invaded Ireland, but in the true malleability of the French spirit, had dwindled from a hero, to a *fille de chambre!*[†] . . . In *l'Hôtel de l'Europe* we stay'd but a couple of days, as a system of cheatery commenc'd, and Lord Mount Cashell was obliged to have recourse to the commissary, on account of extortion. Justice was immediately allotted him. However, we directly removed to *l'Hôtel d'Espagne, Rue de la Loi* at eighteen Louis d'ors a month.

Hôtel d'Espagne, Paris, 1801. Sunday Dec. 13th, or (as they call it here) le dimanche ce 12me Frimaire, An 10.

I have let a week elapse since I wrote last, and now I am come, Bob, open mouth'd, to tell you what I have seen, that is to say, if I can possibly remember.

First we went to the Thuilleries, and walk'd in the gardens, which are ornamented with statues, very well copied from those in the Louvre. The palace of the Thuilleries is magnificent, and the outward adornment of the four iron gates (which inclose a spacious court) are the beautiful and celebrated horses taken

* Former.
† Chambermaid.

from Venice together with four cocks, the French symbol which at first I thought were Roman eagles. We then visited the *Musée Central des Arts*, which is in the Louvre.

As well as being the sanctuary for French, Dutch and German masterpieces of genius it is possess'd of the plunder of Italy. This gallery is open to foreigners every day and to the publick twice a week and like all the other national institutions free of all expense and difficulty of access, which latter circumstance particularly is a most signal blessing! I declare I scarcely know how to set about describing this place to you! it is such an endless exhibition. . . . I am not qualified to do anything more than admire and nothing gives a less defined notion of what you want to convey an idea of, than a violent explosion of one's own wonder.

The Apollo Belvidere extorts nevertheless, a few exclamations. For really, and truly, if one cou'd imagine the perfection of divinity, it is this lovely godlike being, found in the ruins of the antient Antium, near Rome, and after having the world for its spectator, through the lapse of three centuries now commands, if possible, heighten'd tributes of enthusiastic applause, from every individual. . . . So far for the Pythian Apollo.

But before we go upstairs to the gallery of paintings, I must observe it is a thousand pities these statues are so badly arranged. They look like noble emigrants fallen from their high estate, huddling together in some degraded situation. The only one wanting to compleat the collection is the Venus de Medici which has not yet arriv'd. . . .

The Palais Royal is excessively new and entertaining to my fancy. One may give it for its motto 'Spectacles for all ages'. There is not a taste, however refined, or the reverse that cannot here be ministered to, in the most diversified manner. Libraries, restaurateurs, gambling houses, coffee houses, pawnbrokers, jewellers, haberdashers, opticians, ice shops, exhibition rooms for dwarfs and giants, dancing dogs and mountebanks, theatres, chess clubs, etc. etc! I shou'd never stop if I were only to give you the catalogue of its contents.

We have taken only one round and I understand (except at a particular hour) it is not look'd upon as right for ladies to go there. Indeed, I believe it is a haunt for great wickedness. But the incongruities of some groups which I saw, were so excessively droll, 'tis impossible not to be amused, let the place be ever so disgraceful. . . .

We saw many other curiosities, but people, I believe interest you more than places and I want to mention Mr Holcroft,* to whom Lady Mount Cashell had a letter of introduction, and who paid his first visit last Tuesday.

He is between sixty and seventy years of age, apparently a clear-headed sensible man, with coarse features, mellow'd away by thought, which has shed itself thro'out his ugly countenance. He was originally a journey-man shoe-maker, which trade he follow'd till he was five and twenty and since that time, educated himself into what he is.

We went to see Mrs and Miss Holcroft the next day, they were both very young women. The former, a French woman very pretty and lively and speaking both languages equally well. Miss Holcroft enthusiastic, and excessively like her father whom she adores.

We have been reading a translation of his from the German, a little poem call'd *Herman and Dorothea*, pretty enough and simple. But I should have liked it better in rhyme, than in blank verse.

I feel as if I should like to say a hundred bitter things of Holcroft, but I have such a trick of not penetrating into people's characters that I don't like to trust myself. He has been here several times and has enter'd fully into conversation which he seems very fond of. A long enquiry into the nature of truth, into which he enter'd eloquently, struck me as very good. . . .

The same day Holcroft came, a family of the name of Rose walk'd into the room as if they had suddenly step'd off of pedestals. They were the first French ladies I had seen and such was the dress of the three demoiselles that I thought some of the

* Thomas Holcroft (1745–1809), dramatist and radical.

statues out of the Louvre had suddenly caught animation, and were come to return the compliments we had paid them in the morning.

Nothing could look more like a little 'Diana' than Victoire, in light (almost transparent) drapery, no sleeves to her gown but gold chain twisted round the upper part of her arm into the form of a bracelet and her neck entirely seen.

She was remarkably pretty and wore her hair with a crescent like a goddess. Her two sisters were in the same style, but had their hair twisted into long snaky curls, from their foreheads down to their chins, and greas'd with what is call'd antique oil. Madame, their mother, was too much *en bon point* to have such a sylphlike appearance as her daughters. But she did not add to her size by too much covering.

They were all ease and affection of manner. Kiss'd us on both cheeks. Encouraged our speaking French. Offer'd a thousand services, and left us amusingly contented with ourselves, and flatter'd with the hope of their visit being repeated.

'Lord bless me! How pleasant French manners are!' Lady Mount Cashell and I exclaim'd with one accord and I felt as if I should have a hundred prisons to get out of, before I cou'd reach half the ease of those amiable mannered little devils. . . .

I am ready to run wild, at my ignorance of French.

Now! Now! Now! you are just going to say. What I am resolv'd you shall not, because I am going to say it myself, that I am angry with all these pretty, tripping, curly, tinsel'd, shrugging, sparkling little Mademoiselles and Monsieurs, not for their own faults, but mine. . . .

le Dimanche ce 22ᵐᵉ [sic] Frimaire, An 10 – Sunday, Decr. 13th 1801.
You know I told you that we were going to the French opera. I was enchanted really with it, first as being a very splendid *coup d'air*, (tho' I have seen the Haymarket) and secondly and lastly, as exhibiting more grace, dexterity of pointed toes, variety and elegance of attitude and sparkling show of dress, etc., than any spectacle I ever saw in my life.

15

The music is, in the vocal line, very inferior to what we are to hear, but the ballets are enchanting. Vestris,* Dehayes and Mademoiselle Chameroi are wonderful, besides hundreds and hundreds of others fully equal in perfection to those I've mentioned, as far as my judgment goes.

Vestris far outstrips the moderation of grace and therefore I don't like him so much as others. A step (or rather attitude) which is call'd *le Pirouette*, or turning on one leg, while the other foot is almost horizontal with the head, is one of the exploits which he excels in. I had heard of the publick decorum in France and indeed the opera was a striking instance of it, for during the length of the entire performance, not a whisper was to be heard! Every eye was turn'd upon the stage, with most devotional attention.

The *Peuple Souverain* are so tenacious for these observances, even in the most trifling respects, that when I threw my shawl over the side of the box, I was obliged to draw it back immediately, or, as a gentleman whispered to me confidentially, a tumult would have been the melancholy consequence and the performance infallibly suspended.

In a little *loge grillé*, almost over the stage is Bonaparte's box (his private one) where he can see without being seen. Madame Bonaparte's box is finely ornamented with scarlet cloth and gold embroidery fringes, tassels, etc. . . .

We have not seen Bonaparte yet, except adorning 'Reticules', which are a species of little workbag worn by the ladies, containing snuff-boxes, billet-doux, purses, handkerchiefs, fans, prayer-books, bon-bons, visiting tickets, and all the machinery of existence.

His image, in plaster of paris, reigns the monarch of even every gingerbread stall, and you can not buy a bit of barley sugar to cure your cold, without having *le Premier Consul*'s head, in all his heroic laurels, sent down your throat, doing the ignominious

* Marie Auguste Vestris (1760–1842), French ballet dancer.

16

job of a sweep chimney! So true it is, that push'd beyond certain bounds, compliment becomes an insult. . . .

Hotel de Rome, Rue Saint Dominique, Faux-bourg St.
Germain. Sunday – 3rd Jany. 1802. 13 Nivose, An 10.
Yesterday we remov'd to this hotel, where we have delightful accommodations for twenty-five Louis a month. To interest you, in its history, it belong'd in days of yore to Madame la Duchesse de Vallière, Louis xiv's mistress. Our apartments are on the second floor. I will describe them, not for their own sake, but to give you an idea of the allotment in Paris hotels, for the price I have mentioned.

The ante-chamber is an excellent one, large, and warm'd by a stove, made like all the Paris ones, of Sèvres manufacture, a white polish'd sort of china. A large screen shades the repository for wood, nothing else you know being burnt in France. A large ornamented (what we call) patent lamp or cluster of them, in the centre and benches all round, where servants are generally stretch'd in *redingotes* (great coats) and cock'd hats, fast asleep during the visit of their Lady.

From the ante-chamber, you go into the *salle à manger*, which has a stove and fireplace, blue lutestring* window curtains, enormous looking-glass and the floor compos'd of brown polish'd wood like mahogany, laid in lozenge forms, and dryrubb'd so bright that one sometimes hazards the bridge of one's nose (if one happens to have one), and a large deal dinner table, as the cloth is never taken away. This does not stand in the room except at meals.

The windows, which are from top to bottom of the room, open like casements, and from balconys you look into a garden and have a view of the Temple of Mars, and all the grounds, attach'd to the neighbouring hotels, which in spring will be a sheet of green.

From the *salle à manger*, is the drawing room, lined with

* A glossy silk cloth.

17

crimson flower'd damask, and gilded fauteuils and sofas, the room lighted by a handsome cut glass lustre, as is the *salle à manger*, which I left in the dark on that subject.

From the drawing room, you go into Lady Mount Cashell's bedchamber furnish'd with blue damask and gold, fauteuils and sofa of the same, looking-glasses (enormous ones) everywhere.

Then, a very good apartment and closets for the two little girls, the door of which last stands opposite the ante-chamber, with a lobby between.

My room is under Lady Mount Cashell's, and precisely alike, with wardrobes in both, my windows opening out into the garden. There are besides rooms for the servants.

A *traiteur** is in the hotel, from whom we have our dinner every day. The floors are all made of brown polish'd wood, as I described that of the *salle à manger*. This gives no idea of the magnificence of the Paris hotels, some of them which I have been in are like enchanted palaces.

Within this fortnight or three weeks, we have had abundant specimens of plays, balls, *soirées*, *thé's*, etc. The first *thé* was at Monsieur Amoulin's. My first impression was amazement, at beholding the women from fifteen to seventy almost in a state of nature. The petticoat (or train of the gown rather) covers however half the length of the room, which is a most benevolent disposition to display in a country where there are not many carpets. . . .

They seem wonderously fond of displaying their sleeveless arms, encircled by a diamond bracelet, and a glittering crescent on their temples, bound by glossy braids of jet black hair. Others in Juno's bright tiara and leopard mantle, assume the goddess, and deck themselves with cameo Joves. Others chain little dimpled *Cupidons* in golden bondage, round their necks, glittering amongst a thousand wings, and smile in all the consciousness of the prettiness of their allegoric attire. Others bony as skeletons, promiscuously cloath'd in band-box offal, glide gaunt

---

* restaurant-keeper.

18

before one's view, and others all paunch and head (like hour-glasses), sad churchyard emblems of the passing time, prove from the upper empty orb the vacancy that pleasure leaves.

No matter, the manners are universally captivating, and tho' I don't want to tease you by admiring what I know you abhor, yet 'tis worth mentioning as a surprizing fact, that after all the revolutions of this magic lantern country, a drawing room is the same today that it was in the courteous age of Louis XIV. . . . It sounds ridiculous to make national observations, when I have seen so little as yet, but the French at present strike me as eating like gourmands. A most odious custom which they have is spitting about the room, which they certainly do to such an excess, that they look like a parcel of Tritons with eternal water spouts playing from their lips. Sometimes even when the pocket-handkerchief is produc'd, it is such a flag of abomination that one feels little redress from the exchange! I wonder they can be so disgusting!!

This same trick I saw practised at Madame de Soubiran's,* where we went to a brilliant ball, composed of all the nations of the earth.

She receiv'd us with excellent address and polish'd hospitality, which does not overpower one, by saying *not* 'Welcome to *my* home,' but 'Welcome to yours,' and certainly one feels as much at ease, as if it really was so.

She is a very beautiful woman, looking about twenty, but really more than twice that age, and dress'd or rather undress'd to the extent of the Parisian fashion.

A cameo, the most preposterous horn'd head of Jupiter which I at first took for her husband's picture, fasten'd an Indian shawl wove in threads of gold upon one polish'd alabaster shoulder, which then fell in drapery over half her person. The other half was not quite so much disguised.

Suspended by sparkling chains to either ear, hung Greek philosophers in medallion'd cameos, a Solon and a Pericles,

* Madame de Soubiran, wife of General de Soubiran.

19

unheard of by her as solemn legislators, while Socrates with all his morals and philosophy attach'd her zone, and Xenophon and Plato true to his principles, impos'd Athenian bondage on her arms.

She spoke all the European languages, and receiv'd everybody in their own tongue, excepting the Turkish ambassador and his turban'd suite who, however spoke French as well as natives.

His Excellency is a man of very imposing aspect, majestic in his air, and beautiful in his features. Tho' nature has distinguished him with so much dignity, it is not diminish'd by the splendour of his ermined robes of scarlet, high turban, long beard, shawl sash, yellow boots, and diamond dagger. Codrica, his Secretary, who is a Greek, is highly instructed, and seems universally admired.

There was a suite of five or six rooms thrown open. In the one in which we were receiv'd at first, stood a most magnificent pavilion ornamented at the foot of either little flight of steps, which stood at the bottom, with two alabaster sphinxes, crown'd with gilded vases in which were fragrant bouquets of delightful flowers.

A mirror form'd one side of the bed which produced a very beautiful deception, all the company, lustres, green-house plants, antique figures and painted ceilings being reflected again by another looking-glass corresponding at the opposite side of the room.

In one of these apartments a number of dancers were collected and a little orchestra of excellent musicians.

The cotillon, or what they call *la contredanse*, was begun when we enter'd the room, and we press'd in amongst the crowd which incircled the exhibition.

Four pretty young ladies, like sylphs and four young men were glittering in the air, indeed such perfection I never witnessed, but the earnestness of their air and countenances for triumph in the publick mind made one apprehend that science had effectually tumbled from the head into the heels.

After the most brilliant exhibition of grace was at an end, and some stage-dances, half minuet, half cotillon, were finish'd, the walses commenced.

Fifty or sixty couple directly form'd a circle round the room and for the first time, I saw the performance so famed amongst the Germans!

Madame de Soubiran and a beautiful young French man, first struck my attention and astonish'd me so much by the elegance of their movements that I did not perceive the comically incongruous assortments of partners who whirl'd one another throughout the circle. . . .

Suddenly the tune turn'd and from a lazy swing, they all jerk'd away upon their pretty little silver slippers, like people bewitch'd. . . . The invitation which we got for this ball supposes our attendance at that hotel throughout the winter. This is universal in Paris.

There was so much rouge on the cheeks of all the ladies, that handsome as Lady Mount Cashell is, her face look'd pale and cold, like a frosty moon, and as for me you must suppose I was like the devil in the mulligrubs,* or any other phantom you can summon to your addled imagination. Besides we were caparison'd so differently from other people, we look'd as if we took a traveller's prerogative, and providently carried all our goods and chattels upon our backs for safety. . . . I think the men affect the English fashions very much. For Englishmen and French women, were quoted all over the world on the decoration of their persons to the best advantage. However the French men cannot resign their gold ear-rings yet, which from being round and large like carriage wheels, keeps one in a perpetual fright lest their heads should suddenly drive full speed off their shoulders.

I forgot to say there was no supper, but potage, patisserie, cakes, punch, tea, lemonade, etc., continually handing about the room. . . .

* In the sulks.

21

'Tis nonsense to talk of the French being Republicans, I don't think a spark exists amongst them. They are excessively fond of rank, honors, and every etiquette that can distinguish them from the multitude. I have had a thousand instances to strengthen this opinion. However, there is a great independence in the lower ranks of people, that I hear is one of the blessings of the Revolution.

I have never met with any creature, who did not speak with regret of the past and horror of the events which were the consequence of political subversion, but remember I have but three weeks' experience to quote! . . .

This day we spent very agreeably. It was the first time we dined at a French house. When the company were told dinner was served, each lady was conducted into the dining room by a gentleman, which is a very pleasant custom by the by, as nothing vexes me more than stalking out of the room by myself, hearkening to the rustling of my tail. I always fancy the devil is at my heels.

We found a most sumptuous banquet prepared. On each cover the name of a guest was written on a little strip of paper. Lady Mount Cashell was handed out of the room by Monsieur l'Abbé Sièyes,* and I by Monsieur, the son of the house, one of those stupifactions of beings whose wit stole into his head, like a mouse into a mouse trap, but was equally sure of losing its life when it attempted an escape. Consequently he never open'd his lips.

However, another 'Monsieur', who sat on the other side of me made ample reparation and diverted me excessively by his gaiety and politeness.

Amongst a wide extended circle, Madame de Viot (one of the Parisian *belles esprits*) struck my attention. She was pass'd sixty years of age with the ugliest face I ever saw in all my life, like a toad that had been trod upon, compleatly crush'd down to one level. Her person was remarkably pretty, and seem'd as if it had

---

* Emmanuel Joseph Sièyes (1748–1836), French politician.

been born forty years after her features. It was set off to the greatest advantage, but so very much exposed, that one cou'd scarcely perceive she had a body to her gown.

She was glittering in very brilliant images across the table to a member of the Institution, when a servant, hitch'd I believe by one of her blade bones, stumbled and let fall an entire vase of liquid over her uncover'd shoulders. Such a ducking no mortal ever got! It trickled unmercifully down her back and put her neck into such a miserable gooseskin, that all its beauty was demolish'd. The scene became very distressing, for she was obliged to be sopped all over with napkins, and servants, gentlemen, and all became her operators. It seem'd really like a judgment on her for her nakedness, as old women are always duck'd for their crimes, and God forgive me, I cou'd hardly keep my countenance.

But a French woman is never put off her guard. This *belle esprit* kept herself perfectly unembarrass'd, and said so many good-humour'd, patient, pleasant entertaining things, that every-body was charm'd with her *esprit*, and really, if she had been a Venus risen from the waves, she cou'd not have receiv'd more sincere admiration than she did for her address, tho' past sixty years of age and exhibited after a ducking. These French people are excessively good-natured and, really, this little circumstance was a good touchstone to the manners of a company. . . .

Sunday, 31st Jan. 1802. Le Dimanche, Pluviose 11ᵐᵉ. Paris, Hotel de Rome, Rue St. Dominique: Fauxbourgs St. Germain.
Time, you know, like everything else is revolutioniz'd here. Instead of the week, they count by the decade.

'But a sixpenny Almanac will tell me this' I think I hear you awfully rejoin. . . .

But we must talk of Bonaparte, whom we saw from one of the windows of the Thuilleries, reviewing his troops just under our eyes, surrounded with his beautiful aides de camps, in hussar cloaks and gold cloth and tassels.

Bonaparte rode on a white charger dressed in the grand

costume of office, which was scarlet velvet richly embroidered with gold. He looked as pale as ashes, and the expression of his countenance was stern severity. His hair is dark, which he wears without powder and his person, which is remarkably small, appears perfectly proportion'd. Except the national cockade, he wore no ornament in his hat, which circumstance distinguish'd him from all the others, whose hats were great repositories for brocade and grandeur.

The Consular guards are the finest set of men I ever saw, all six feet high and each, 'tis said, owes his appointment to some signal act of valour. Their uniform is blue, turn'd up with white, and edged with red and on their heads, a high furr cap, with brazen plates. The dragoons are Green Dragons, and look very fine, – but the Egyptian Mamelukes, on Arabian coursers, struck my fancy most, from the uncommon splendour of their appearance. All the regiments saluted Bonaparte and (not to enter farther into the detail of military proceedings which I certainly don't comprehend), the entire spectacle was extremely brilliant and I was more gratified than I ever was by a warlike pageant in all my life. . . .

Miss Berry, more critical than Katherine in this instance, thought very differently. '. . . all I could observe was that they never marched in straight lines, and that their muskets were carried in various directions; any of our colonels of militia would have been ashamed of their men so marching before the king.'[1]

There was more unanimity as to Napoleon's appearance: 'a little man', commented Miss Berry 'remarkably well on horseback, with a sallow complexion, a highish nose, a very serious countenance and cropped hair.'[2]

Others had also noted him, among them the brother of the British Plentipotentiary, 'his figure is well proportioned his features are handsome, complexion rather sallow, hair very dark, cut short and without powder. He has fine eyes full of spirit and intelligence, a firm severe mouth, indicating a stern and inflexible will, in a word you see in his countenance, the master mind. . . .'[3]

Another witness saw 'the terror of the great part of Europe . . . lodged in a small light body about five feet four inches high which was covered by an ill-made crimson velvet coat with gold lace and embroidery on the collar and sleeves; white pantaloons and boots. . . . His countenance appeared to be thin, sallow and unhealthy. The lightening of his eye which is so often talked of was not then flashing nor was there anything in his appearance which would have led me to suppose that he was anything more than an attorney's clerk.'[4]

We have repeated our attendance at the houses I have mentioned and, as Lord Mount Cashell is a subscriber to *Le Salon des Etrangers*, we went to the famous subscription ball held in *la Rue Grange Batelière*. . . .

We arriv'd there in due rotation about one in the morning, the police being so strict that no confusion is permitted by allowing one carriage to take precedence of another. I will not describe the scene of festivity otherwise to you, than as it gave us an opportunity of seeing Madame Tallien,* Madame Viscomti, Genl. Berthier's mistress, and ladies of that notoriety whose fame excites one's vagabond curiosity, and who one cou'd never meet in Parisian society as their mal-practices throw them totally out of private notice.

There was something in Madame Tallien's air and appearance that absolutely transfix'd me to the spot where she was. Even before I knew that it was she, I was caught by the most enchanting smile I ever saw, which led me to examine from whom it proceeded. The lady, when she no longer smiled, was far from arresting one's attention, where there were so many beautiful claimants, but in waiting to catch another smile, I found a thousand attractions crowd upon my view.

She had the sweetest expression of mildness and good temper and a modest mien of domestic habits, with that fair delicacy of appearance that instantly struck me. She wore no rouge and yet

* Jeanne Marie Tallien (1773–1835). Charming hostess of the *nouveaux riches* in Paris whose parties 'disgusted' Richard Lovell Edgeworth.

look'd fresh and lovely! I cannot describe to you my astonishment at hearing it was the all-renowned Madame Tallien, who I had pictured to my imagination as dashing, intrepid and dazzling like the meridian sun. But no French woman is dashing, nor none attempts to take your admiration by storm, tho' they don't seem to understand what *mauvaise honte** means. . . .

About a fortnight ago, we were at a superb entertainment at Mr Smith's, American ambassador to Portugal, now at Paris for his diversion. There was music of the sweetest kind, the horn and harp accompanying the vocal performers. We were introduced to Madame de Staël-Holstein,[†] Necker's daughter, who in appearance reminded me very much of Lady Granard. We were also introduced to Helen Maria Williams,[‡] to the family of Livingston, the American minister from the United States to Paris, to the Princess de Belmonte, a Neapolitan lady, Russian Princesses, and a thousand others. This night ended with a most magnificent supper.

Miss Williams is in perpetual mourning for her sister. She wears, added to her black dress, a long black gauze scarf thrown over her head, and hanging down to her feet. I never saw manners so desirous to please, as hers, nor a countenance more corresponding to this idea. She speaks in a tone of voice that sounds like an invalid and tho' large in her person, a general air of languor reigns throughout her exterior.

We were invited to her house the day after our introduction. Her family consists of an old Scotch, high-blooded lady, her mother, two little nephews and their father, a young Frenchman. Mr Stone[§] is also their inmate, it was he who befriended

---

* False modesty.

† Germaine de Staël (1766–1817), celebrated writer and salon hostess.

‡ Helen Maria Williams (1762–1827), English author and poetess, settled in Paris in 1790 and was imprisoned by Robespierre.

§ John Hurford Stone (1763–1818), Maria Williams' lover, and an Englishman of Republican principles.

Charlotte Corday* on her tryal.

He is an Englishman, and one of the most sensible ones I ever saw. Their hotel is in the midst of a delightful garden and we spent the evening in her library, which was particularly corresponding with her style of society, the latter being compos'd of senators, members of the National Institute, in their blue embroider'd coats, and every one in the literary line. We have a general permission to frequent these societies twice every week and they will, I dare say, present us with various specimens of natural curiosities. . . . Last Friday we went to a French ball, then to a grand one at the American ambassador's and so ended the night at the masquerade. This implys the carnival has begun and all the people are running wild after amusement. But they are only making preparations, for the grand days of exhibition will not take place for a week or more.

I never was at a masquerade before in my life. It was at the opera house, and half over when we enter'd, a dozen of us in our dominos altogether. Lady Mount Cashell and I were attack'd by a gentleman, for ladies only wore masks and as Lady Mount Cashell chose to pass for a man, from the prerogative of her height, all the flirtation fell upon my shoulders. I pretended to be a Turkish lady, under the dragon influence of my husband who was Lady Mount Cashell. He commiserated on me being under the subjection of a tyrant, as a Turk must naturally be, and in the most gallant language proposed to snap my chains, etc.

As for characters supported well, I saw very few indeed, tho' the scene was excessively gay, the numbers absolutely without end and the whole conducted with inconceivable propriety. Novelty is opening before our eyes in a thousand shapes, and tho' I have a brace of eyes in my head on very hard duty yet I never think of a peacock without envy, for having so many useless ones in his tail. . . .

In dining out yesterday, I was much diverted at a little

---

* Marie Anne Charlotte Corday d'Armont (1768–93), the murderess of the tyrant, Marat.

accident that happened to the Turkish ambassador by whom I was sitting at dinner. He was in the act of explaining to me some customs in Constantinople, when a bottle of champagne burst with so much violence that some heretical drops of wine sprinkled his Mahometan ermined sleeve. Really, I never saw anything so dreadful as a Turk in a passion!! His eyes flash'd forth fire, and I thought he would have been tempted to draw his diamond dagger upon the unlucky offender.

After deprecating the Prophet's wroth, by mumbled expiations, he strode into the drawing-room, with his robes flying wide behind him, like a tragic king and seated himself cross-legg'd upon the sofa, after having flung his yellow slippers on the floor. There he held himself in deepest meditation for an hour, and on seeing us amusing ourselves by quaffing liqueurs and coffee, to my amazement he started up and drank down without stopping six glasses of the strongest liqueurs upon the board. He then walk'd with measured pace about the room, call'd all his merry musselmen about him, and departed to offer to Mahomed the contaminated robe as a sacrifice to appease his vengeance. This is a literal fact, for I heard him say so myself 'with my own ears'. . . .

The next day we spent the morning at Monsieur Pougence, where we saw a thousand curiosities in the book line. We were also introduced to a niece of Lavater's,* who is also a physiognomist, a comical looking little woman in a bright yellow wig and inheriting a great deal of her uncle's enthusiasm on the same subject. She gave some good guesses with respect to Lady Mount Cashell's character from her countenance.

That day we dined amongst a diplomatic set, at the American ambassador's and for the first time saw the Minister of the Exterior, Talleyrand,† Lucasina, the Prussian ambassador, General Berthier, Minister of war. . . .

---

* Johann Kaspar Lavater (1741–1801), writer on physiognomy.

† Charles Maurice De Talleyrand-Perigord (1754–1838). Brilliant diplomat and statesman.

General Berthier* in the full national uniform walk'd in a slovenly gait across the room, and handed Lady Mount Cashell into dinner. He is a little slouch'd looking man, brusque in his manners, and abrupt in his address. Talleyrand then came towards me to perform the like ceremony. He moved paunch foremost in his scarlet velvet embroidered official coat, bag and ruffles. At a distance, his face is large, pale and flat, like a cream cheese, but on approaching nearer, cunning and rank hypocrisy supplant all other resemblances.

On sitting down to dinner, he spoke on different subjects politely enough and mentioned his having been in England, on the presumption of my being an English woman. I told him I was Irish, and the word seem'd to revive some remembrance of successful perfidy. For when he repeated with surprise *'Comment! Mademoiselle est Irlandaise!'* a diabolical gleam lit the expanse of his face with such a smile as I never desire to see, as long as I live, again.

Just then after dismissing his soup, he enter'd with interest upon his dinner and certainly such a gourmandeur never was it before my fate to behold. For the length of two hours, his mouth was never closed, and even at the intervals of plate changing he fill'd up crevices by demolishing a dish of raw artichokes, in his neighbourhood. Oh! such a cormorant! . . .

---

* Alexander Berthier (1753–1815), Marshal of France and Minister of War.

13 March – 13 October 1802

13 March, 1802.   22 Ventose – Hotel de Rome, Rue St. Dominique, Fauxbourgs St. Germain.

A month has passed since I last wrote. Within the last week the town has been compleatly a masquerade. The carnival has commenced some time, and all is universal jubilee. One meets nothing but bears on horseback, priests, harlequins, mercurys, monkeys, gods, goddesses and long-tail'd devils, riding, driving, running and dancing about the streets.

A few mornings ago, while Lord and Lady Mount Cashell and myself were sitting at breakfast, the door open'd and a young man appear'd, who immediately flew towards me, and kiss'd me with the utmost cordiality.

As none of us had ever recollected to have seen him before, you may imagine our consternation! Till on his bursting out laughing, and asking 'if it was possible we did not recollect him the night before at the ball'? It proved to be an electioneering manner'd little Dutch woman, who wanted to run up two or three rungs higher in the ladder of society, and took the means of paying her visits *en garçon* knowing it was a practice not in use amongst us.

She had follow'd her husband to the wars and fought at his side during the campaign. Whenever she went out to walk, it was as I describe. But the practice is common in Paris of women wearing men's cloaths. A ceremony however is necessary to go through which is to take out a written permission from one of the publick offices of government. Madame shewd us her's in which it was legally granted in all its formalities. The little girls, till they are eleven or twelve years old most frequently dress *en garçon*. They imagine it is a less cumbersome cloathing than petticoats and that it leaves the limbs more at ease. . . .

30

At the publick balls, I often see pretty nice little girls dress'd as boys, and dancing most beautifully. They don't simplify the cloaths of children half so well as in England.

A child of five years old, when they do wear petticoats, is the precise miniature of her mama. Her hair dressed *à la grec*, her gown close to her form and a long train of which she has the conduct, so as to dispose of it in the most graceful manner. 'Tis laughable the airs these little babies give themselves, in imitating every action of their mothers! So that since they *will* make them little apes when they dress them in petticoats 'tis better they shou'd manage them as they do.

All the children I have seen are so carressing in their manners, it really delights one. For women to be good mothers is quite the fashion, and we have been taken up on tiptoe to look at the little creatures alseep in the nursery, in the very midst of the ball, when the Mama has returned back again to receive the homage of her admirers, and interchange their billet doux. One often sees children foolishly brought to the theatres. Ladies frequently nurse their infants themselves and Madame Tallien is famous in this way.

While I am on the subject of domestic qualities, I must add, that it is so much the fashion for husbands and wives to seem to love one another, that I have seen *Monsieur le mari*, hand his wife into a room, and sit at her elbow half the evening, at the very time arrangements were making for a divorce. They are quite at home in publick and some people say the contrary of this holds good. But I am not enough domesticated in any family yet to be able to judge of the truth of the remark. . . .

Sunday 25th April, 1802. 5me Florial.   Hotel de Rome, Rue St. Dominique, Fauxbourgs St. Germain.
I have six weeks to account for, and having let so much time pass unmethodiz'd, it seems to have diffused itself in nothingness like a bankless stream.

One thing I however recollect, that we went with Mr Livingston, son to the American Minister, to see Tom Payne.*

* Thomas Paine (1737–1809), Republican and author of the famous *Rights of Man*.

31

Our excuse for so doing was his new constructed bridge, which he has made a model of, and which is his hobby-horse at present.

He lives up half a dozen flight of stairs, in a remote part of the town. He receiv'd us with the greatest good humour, and instantly set about exhibiting his playthings. Besides this model, he has various others and is at present planning a method of building houses, without permitting the damp to penetrate.

A friend of his lives in the house with him, whose two little boys, children of four and five years old, he has adopted. During the entire morning that we spent with him, they were playing about the room, overturning all his machinery and putting everybody out of patience except himself, who exhibited the most incorrigible good temper.

His appearance is plain beyond conception. Drinking spirits has made his entire face as red as fire and his habits of life have render'd him so neglectful in his person that he is generally the most abominably dirty being upon the face of the earth. He complimented us with a clean shirt, and with having his face washed, which Mr Livingston said was one of the greatest efforts he ever was known to make.

In spite of his surprizing ugliness, the expression of his countenance is luminous, his manners easy and benevolent, and his conversation remarkably entertaining. Vanity is his ruling passion, and praise in any way infatuates him.

He introduced some little poems of his own composition, the title of one was *The Castle in the Air* and, in the fanciful style, I really think they were the most elegant things I ever heard, tho' the occasion was ridiculous, for they were address'd to a lady who he had persuaded himself was in love with him and whom he offended so much by the supposition, that they were written to produce a reconciliation.

In the course of conversation he alluded to his works and recounted various anecdotes, which happened at coffee-houses, in consequence of their being discuss'd before his face. Altogether his style of manner is guileless and good-natured, and I was agreeably disappointed in him, considering the odiously disagreeable things I was led to expect. . . .

So now to talk to you of the re-establishment of the Roman Catholick Religion in France.* Easter Sunday, 18th of this month, all the world assembled at *l'église de Notre Dame* to witness the resurrection of the publick faith which had slept with its holy fathers during the long period of the French Revolution.

The aisles were all hung throughout with Gobelins tapestry, and in the most conspicuous parts were erected two canopies of crimson and gold, towering with plumes of white feathers.

After the priests had burnt incense before him on his entrance, Bonaparte appear'd under one of these canopies with the two consuls attending, and guarded by a host of generals, and Cardinal Caprara, the Pope's legate, occupied the other, encircled by bishops and archbishops, priests and deacons, in all the holy gradations of apostolic precedence.

The *Te Deum* was the grandest thing I ever heard, and the musical performers scattered throughout the church, so that the choruses fill'd the entire place and seem'd but one voice.

All the bishops were install'd, and solemnly sworn at the foot of Bonaparte, and the devotional reverence they pay'd to him, was almost on a par with their eucharistical worship.

These godly fopperies continued during seven hours, and the three consuls return'd in procession under a sort of Chinese canopy, supported by obsequious priests. Cardinal Caprara, in his gold mitre and papal robes, administered to himself the sacrament, and then solemnly dismiss'd us with a musical benediction. Madame Bonaparte, and all her court added much to the gaudiness of the scene, as she was a blaze of diamonds, and all the ladies throughout caparisoned with corresponding splendour.

The foreign ministers, the strangers of rank, the men in office, etc., sat confess'd on crimson benches dress'd in their golden embroidery and the bishops paraded in white satin shoes tinsell'd with silver, white gloves and sparkling rings glittering on their fingers outside the gauntlets, so that they gave me the notion of fell enchanters, who through the witchery of their spells and necromancy caused a resurrection of the departed

* The substitution of the Republican for the Gregorian calendar and the establishment of the secular Feasts of Reason had taken place on 19 November 1793.

spirit of the Roman Catholic religion, as a new species of passtime to Bonaparte the king, and made the phantom flit before his eyes in all the changes of the gaudiest pageantry.

In the evening we walk'd in the gardens of the Thuilleries. The palace and all the buildings, trees, bridges, etc. were illuminated and look'd like enchanted castles of fire, and the waterworks reflected thousands of these in their spray, dancing in the most vivid colours. . . .

*David** is worth mentioning, whom we have seen often at his house in the Louvre. He was the bloody adherent of Robespierre, and I believe to this moment maintains the justice of his practices.

He is terrific in his appearance, and not unlike what his friend was described to be, after having made an attempt against his life, and when he was leading to the scaffold.

His mouth is dreadfully distorted and turn'd almost into one cheek, so that his jaw teeth are discoverable to the front. I can't describe to you the carnivorous aspect this produces. His eyes are not inexpressive of better qualities than his actions teach us to believe him capable of, and when he is pleased, his manners are not unpleasant. His picture of the *Sabines* is reckon'd good, and his *Horatii* and *Brutus* are much spoken of. I have seen them all, but am not going to torment you with any description.

Versailles, May 16th, 1802.   25 Florial.
I have been a resident here three weeks, and certainly my star peep'd from beneath its cloud in conducting me to the house of Monsieur and Madam de Pescheloche.

The advantage of being in a French family, is what has tempted me away from Lady Mount Cashell for a month, and one week more of purgatory remains before I rejoin her at Paris.

If it was not for the privation of her society, I shou'd recoil at stigmatising this abode by such a term. For were one to search through the world with a lantern in one's hand, one cou'd not

---

* Jacques Louis David (1749–1825), founder of the modern French School of Painting.

34

find better specimens of humanity than Monsieur and Madame de Pescheloche. They have been bred up in the best society, and through the adversity of the Revolution, have exchanged the superfluities of wealth for all the stamina of wisdom and all the chearfulness of mild tranquility. Monsieur de Pescheloche commands at Versailles. He is *Chef d'Escadron* in the 1st Regt of Cavalry. . . .

There is another *Chef d'Escadron*, Monsieur Mongein, in the same regiment, and who is perpetually our inmate. He is by no means an uninform'd man, but the most eccentric French man I have ever seen. His passion is war and his appearance is precisely that of Charles xııth, King of Sweden. Tho' he never wears anything but the national uniform, he always gives me the idea of his being in full armour.

He has served in all the Italian campaigns and never was known to yield in any single instance to the habitual practices of General Massena* in the way of plunder and depredation. On the contrary, he was chivalrous in befriending the vanquish'd and his character was so well known, that he was apply'd to on every occasion on the part of the enemy, when sacking towns, villages, etc., threw them particularly at the mercy of the French.

His being perfectly unconscious of his own generous disposition, almost inclines one to forgive his everlastingly talking of battle and bloodshed, fire and sword, death and destruction, till he intoxicates himself with the idea of his being absolutely oppos'd against the enemy and strides across the room with the same airs as if he was going to raise the siege of a town.

On these occasions, he generally treads on the tail of poor Bellotte, Madame de Pescheloche's lap-dog, or overturns the trick-track tables, or catches his spur in the train of one's gown, which brings him back to his senses again. Then he looks down into the crown of his helmet with as much confusion as if he had committed a crime against the state, of the most disgraceful

* André Masséna, Duke of Rivoli, Prince of Essling (1756–1871), the greatest of Napoleon's marshals.

nature. Altogether he is the greatest curiosity I ever saw in my life. . . .

I have got by heart most of the environs of Versailles. We subscribe to the Petit Trianon, where we often walk in the evenings. This was the favourite retreat of Marie Antoinette, and one of the loveliest little spots in the world. At present the grass is yellow with cowslips, the almond trees blossoming, cherry, lilacs, honeysuckles, etc., in full bloom and perfume, and the air enbalm'd wherever one moves.

The palace here is superb. I have frequently walk'd through it to see the paintings, apartments etc., which are very grand, and interest one from being so much connected with the story of the Revolution. They shew the door where the Queen made her escape, the *orangerie* where the Swiss were hid etc.

The park is magnificent but quite in the old fashion'd style of gardening. Temples dedicated to Apollo, to Proserpine, to Venus, to Cupid and Psyche, all made of polish'd white marble, and embellish'd with lamps, *jets d'eau*, dragons, frogs, and every incongruity that fancy can devise. Thickly interspersed throughout the endless avenues of clipp'd chestnuts, oaks, poplars, etc. are placed statues of all the mob of heaven, and in geometrical lakes, are centred brazen allegories of mythologic lore.

However degraded the taste of Louis xiv's age, Versailles strikes the eye of a stranger with infinite grandeur, from its great dimensions and peculiar accordance with high aristocratical ideas of kingly magnificence. . . .

I am tired absolutely of talking out of doors. If you have a mind, I will tell you how the interior is regulated, as this is the first time I have lived literally in a French family, and for the first few days I felt as ridiculously circumstanc'd as the devil when he tumbled headlong into the holy water.

The first of this month (May), Madame de Pescheloche woke me by laying a bunch of flowers upon my pillow, which is the custom of the country. Then to proceed in the detail of the day. Monsieur gets up very early and settles his regimental affairs, smokes, and eats his breakfast before eight o'clock. Madame and I, then go to the bath, and do not return to our breakfast till ten or eleven o'clock. I observe when any gentlemen call in the morning, Monsieur de Pescheloche gives them out of a little silver cup, a *pièce* of liqueurs.

Work, reading, riding or walking fills up the space till dinner. By that time, what with the stimulants of coffee, snuff, liqueurs, baths and compliments, we are in high good humour, and begin our soup without much appetite, then eat our *bouilli* to produce one, then demolish our *légumes*, then encourage ourselves a little with our *fricandeaux,* and at length begin with earnestness on our *rôti*. Patisserie, omelette, confitures etc. succeed in slow rotation, till after an hour and a half *la sallade* and *le petit dessert*, announce the termination of the repast.

Coffee succeeds, which I think the best part of the story, and walking or cards, or in short whatever occupies us in the evening, is shared in common, as ladies and gentlemen never think of separating or finding any amusement out of one another's society. We go to bed at about eleven, and Monsieur de Pescheloche sees me into my room with my candle in his hand, and looks about to see that everything is comfortable. He then wishes me good night in his solemn manner and ends with *'Adieu Mademoiselle! Dormez bien.'*

I was over-fatigued the other day with riding, and the next morning stay'd in bed with the headache, when what was my consternation, at seeing Monsieur de Pescheloche, in full regimentals dress'd for parade, quietly stealing into my room with my bason of coffee in his hand. He thought I was asleep, because I did not speak, and very tidily got a little table and left my breakfast for me, at my bedside. I mention these little circumstances to mark the difference of manners and customs.

When I was here a fortnight, Lord and Lady Mount Cashell, Mr Parnell and Lord King* came to Versailles, to take me back to Paris for a few days. The object was our presentation to Madame

* Peter, 7th Baron King of Ockham (1776–1833).

Bonaparte. They spent the day here, and we all dined together at the Inn. . . .

This was the only day I ever knew to turn out pleasantly when the parties were forewarn'd they were to like one another. But it really was delightful and we all set off for Paris as gay as larks. And the next day, at three o'clock, Lady Mount Cashell and I drove off in state to the Thuilleries to be presented to Madame Bonaparte.

The room was crowded and Madame Bonaparte was seated on a sofa, when Mr Merry, our Minister, brought us up, to make our obeisance before her. She is that sort of looking woman, that if chance had not placed her on such a pinnacle, would escape minute observation. Her manners are gentlewomanlike, amiable and pleasing, and her reception of us was easy and excessively polite. After staying a quarter of an hour, she rose, made a regal courtesy and withdrew. Everybody then drove about Paris, making visits to the House of Bonaparte, Lucien, Louis etc., and the prefect of the palace. This ended the business and this incense to royalty is administered every month. . . .

Paris, Hotel de Rome, Rue St. Dominique, Fauxbourgs Saint Germain, 1802. Sunday, 19th June, 30 Prairel.
A week after I wrote last, I left Versailles accompanied by Lord and Lady Mount Cashell, who came to take me back to Paris. My parting with Monsieur and Madame de Pescheloche was quite a serious operation. Their affection and good-nature to me was so peculiar. . . . Madame de Pescheloche and I are to be correspondents for life, and we amuse ourselves with the notion of writing dispatches, she perch'd on the summit of the Pyrenees, and I on the top of the Alps. For you know our destination is to spend next winter in Italy.

But I must return John-trot to my journal. The circumstances which have lately occurr'd in this household are the arrival of Mrs Ruaud, as governess to the girls, and Mr Egan with the three elder boys* from Ireland. This month's absence of mine

* The children of Lord and Lady Mount Cashell.

has made Paris quite different, our family is so large. The weather is oppressive and scorching. Such multitudes of English as have arriv'd, and all the balls and gaieties at an end. . . .

The fifth of this month we dined at the Thuilleries with Bonaparte. After passing through various ante-chambers where were bands of military music, we at length reach'd the room where Madame Bonaparte sat under a canopy blazing in purple and diamonds. More than two hundred persons were assembled and Bonaparte walk'd about the room speaking politely to everybody. His countenance is delightful when animated by conversation, and the expression in the lower part of his face pleasing to the greatest degree. His eyes are reflection itself, but so charming a smile as his, I never scarcely beheld. His dress was simple and his air, tho' reserv'd, announcing everything of the polish'd gentleman.

The band struck up on our going in to dinner, to which Bonaparte led the way by taking the regal prerogative of walking out of the room first. Everyone follow'd indiscriminately and both Bonaparte and Madame sat down at the side of the table without any regard to place. Lady Mount Cashell, looking beautiful and dress'd in black crape and diamonds, was handed in to dinner by the English Minister, and I by General Grouchy,* Madame Condorcet's brother, a highly polish'd and pleasing man.

He was my society during dinner, for on looking to my right hand, who should I see gobbling like a duck but Talleyrand. We however renew'd our acquaintance for two or three minutes, and then I left him, to the destruction of all the poultry he could lay his claw upon.

General Grouchy was second in command in the affair of Bantry Bay,† on board the *Fraternité*, and had every intention of

* Emmanuel de Grouchy (1766–1847), Marshal of France.

† In December 1796 the French had threatened an invasion of Ireland in sympathy with the anti-British activities of the United Irishmen.

snapping the grappling irons which attach Ireland to England.

We laugh'd heartily at the different circumstances under which our acquaintance wou'd have commenc'd had the business succeeded. However, I took care to tell him, had their philanthropic undertaking prosper'd as happily in Ireland as it did across the Alps, I should expect by this time to see our little island hung up as a curiosity in the Louvre amongst the Italian trophies.

This would not have been too civil, but that it past in the highest good spirits. He had just been admiring Lady Mount Cashell, and in allusion to that said it was not necessary to go to Italy to look for Venus's and Apollo's, etc.

I was more regaled than I can express by the perfume of oranges and roses which, with a thousand other kinds of flowers, seem'd to grow out of moss and artificial rocks, the entire length of the plateau which reach'd from the top to the bottom of the table. There was a servant to every chair and nothing but plate was used. The apartments were hung over with fine Gobelins, and the ceilings painted by the first hands. Grecian statues brought out of Italy ornamented the room where we dined and musick play'd delightfully during the entire entertainment.

After sitting two hours, we return'd into the reception room, drank coffee and liqueurs, talk'd in coteries, and so departed after having spent an uncommonly amusing day. But I believe there never was a court more manacled by the observances of etiquette, than the Thuilleries.

Lady Mount Cashell and I are in the carriage almost every morning at seven o'clock, and drive off to Tivoli, where the establishment for bathing is on the most extensive scale. One may have baths prepared in imitation of every kind of water in the world and drink the factitious ones, with equal effect.

We only bathe in common warm-water. But the Ladies most frequently have their baths perfum'd with eau de Cologne, rose water, or some perfume of that kind.

The little garden into which every bath opens is absolutely red with roses, and the women who attend, cleanly dress'd every morning in a white linen jacket and petticoat. It is very much the fashion to breakfast in the bath, and we sometimes call for our *cotelette en papillote*, potage or whatever else we like, for the variety of *déjeuners* are inexhaustible. Afterwards we walk frequently in the public gardens, which are very fine and a part of the establishment of Tivoli. But it would be endless to describe publick gardens, as at present Paris seems but to peep from amongst its green leaves 'like the Devil in a bush'.

The boulevards, which encircle the town, are thickly planted with high branching trees, under which is an eternal scene of festivity. All the cafés are out of doors, and a thousand groups of happy looking people, sitting under blossoming arbours, quaffing lemonade, wine, cider or beer, and conducting themselves with such chearfulness and decorum, that it is delightful to witness it.

The little cabarets are full of dancers. The theatres for the People are open everywhere and amusement of this nature purchasable at five Sous. Musick breathes universally throughout. The trees on either side of the boulevard meet like an arch at top, and a thousand lamps sparkle through the branches.

The oratory of charlatans! the tricks of conjurers! the particolour'd limbs of harlequins that you catch flourishing in the air! the eternal balance of the network swing-swang! the long bounding of the tight-rope! with a hundred such fooleries, serve to diversify the scene and give an indiscribable effect of innocent festivity! . . .

The moon was beautifully bright and the summer lightning so mingled with fire-works, that 'twas difficult to distinguish the difference. Suddenly the heavens appear'd open'd, the thunder broke over our heads, and the fork'd-flashes of lightning gave so livid an effect to every creature that you wou'd have imagin'd a church-yard was suddenly brought to life. The bolts fell from heaven amongst the crowd, and in a moment, everyone disappeared and flew in consternation to the houses, as tho' they had relaps'd into their sepulchres. So far for the fluctuation

41

of climates. But these French people possess the genius of amusing themselves beyond anything I ever saw, and they mingle throughout their entertainments a spirit of attraction, that bewitches everybody at the time into a total forgetfulness that there exists anything in the world more agreeable, or more delightful than themselves!!!

Paris, 30th July, 1802.   9 Thermidor, Hotel de Rome, Rue St. Dominique.
A month has slipt through my fingers and I feel very much at a loss to account for its expenditure. . . .

In fact the month had been consumed by anxiety occasioned by the arrival of Lady Mount Cashell's seventh child. It says much for that remarkable woman that she had been pregnant throughout their visit to France, though this may have been prearranged to preserve her from the attentions of the Earl.

For as she remarked in her memoirs, 'the further I travelled the more contemptible Lord M's character appeared; however though I often wished to be liberated from his company, I loved my children too well to make any positive effort for a separation which had been more than once talked of but never seriously discussed.'[1]

Nevertheless she apparently 'felt less regard for him every day', a circumstance which must have considerably added to Catherine's burden of keeping the domestic peace.

The 25th of June, Lady Mount Cashell added a *citoyen* to the French Republick. Two days after his birth he was presented to the Municipality and his name inscrib'd in the national archives. This ceremony is necessary with everyone born in France, and it may be an advantage in giving him constitutional rights, as long as he lives, if the French have any such to impart, which seems to be much doubted. . . .

Lady Mount Cashell's confinement will best account to you for the want of incident in this last month, which has not been much spent beyond the precincts of her bed-chamber.

I forgot to mention Mr Fox* with whom at Miss Williams' we spent the evening. He was paid great compliment and attention, but was rather lourd and maladroit in his address and embarrass'd in his manners. As he did not enter into conversation with those he was presented to, I can only say of him, that the vision I had of the Great Man, disappointed me most dolefully.

Paris, 30th August, 1802 – Hotel de Rome; Rue St. Dominique, Fauxbourgs St. Germain. 15 Fructidor.
Lady Mount Cashell is at length beginning to reassume her usual habits of life . . . on the subject of mothers and sons, I must tell you Lady Mount Cashell has been occupying herself in having her's christened. There has been a glorious junketting of course, the gossips being the Polish Countess Myscelska, the American Minister and Mr William Parnell. The name of the child is Richard Francis Stanislaus Moore.

This godmother of his is a very amiable being. She has just arriv'd at that unbounded extent of aristocracy which always produces the utmost republicanism of manners, and with more than regal revenues, she is the most simple and unpretending of any one in society.

The other day she call'd in here, and saw Lady Mount Cashell eating plain boil'd potatoes for her luncheon in the middle of the day. She then heard for the first time that *that* was the principal food of the Irish, and immediately resolv'd on giving Lady Mount Cashell a breakfast in compliment to her country. We went there and literally found nothing but potatoes dress'd in fifty different fashions. I thought the repast would never have been at an end, such was the torture she had put her fancy to in divising methods to diversify the cookery.

She has insisted on Lady Mount Cashell making her a present of a tree, which Lady Mount Cashell has, choosing an arbutus as being common in Ireland. She is to take it into Poland with her where she has a little plantation representative of her friends

* The Hon. Charles James Fox (1749–1806), statesman and orator.

43

and favourites, each having given her the sort of tree most emblematic of their sentiment towards her, and in this place she walks, and imagines herself conversing with all she loves, and likes, in every corner of the world.

She has four or five little children, and their education is her chief hobby-horse. It is a curiosity to peep into the establishment of her house. She has studied the nature of each child and has provided tutors according with the disposition, so that there is no end of instructors. Every language they are to learn introduces a new inmate into the family, and you really wou'd suppose you were in the Tower of Babel if you were but to spend half an hour in her drawing room. . . .

Within the last week Lord Mount Cashell and Mr Moore have set out on an expedition to Orleans. We have late in the evenings under the escort of two or three gentlemen, gone vagabondizing on the boulevards, and poking our noses into every haunt of the lower order of people. We have been in cabarets, cafés, 'theatres' where you pay a few sous for entrance, in the midst of dancing dogs, conjurers, wild beasts, puppet shews, charlatans, gangues,* and in short every resort where the manners of the people cou'd be characteriz'd, and I protest for the motto of the meanest place, you may put 'Elegant Decorum', without the least fear of these expressions being forfeited in the most trifling instance. . . .

It would be interesting to know who were the 'two or three gentlemen' who went 'vagabondizing' with Katherine and Lady Mount Cashell as soon as Lord Mount Cashell's back was turned. As it was, the nine months' visit to Paris was now drawing to a close, and a winter in Italy lay before them.

In the short time left the friends made several excursions, among them to the romantic ruins of the Château of Meudon, where Katherine indulged her Gothic taste exploring 'the Square Courts and ruin'd pavements where wildness and neglect mark'd every footstep'.[2] They

* Gangs.

44

met Mrs Opie,* 'who writes poems and novels'; supped several times with the actor, John Kemble. Sad to leave Paris, they comforted themselves they would be returning there before going back to Ireland. They didn't know it, but they would never see it together again.

Thursday, 23 Sep. 1802 – Roanne – 3 Vendemiaire, An 11. Department of the Rhone et Loire.

For fear this shou'd meet you in a methodical mood, I will begin our journey by telling you how we were all dispos'd of, and stow'd away, in the different carriages, this day week when we bid adieu to Paris.

Mrs Ruaud and her two children, Helena and Jane, Mr Egan, Robert and Edward, with the children's maid, Mary Lawless, set off in the coach a day before us, as accommodations were not likely to be found at the inns for so large a party. William the groom rode courier to this expedition. Lady Mount Cashell and the little infant, in its cradle, and Mary Smith then pack'd themselves in the chaise, and Lord Mount Cashell, Kilworth,[†] and I in a French-carriage purchas'd for the occasion. To this party, Para in his gold-trimm'd blue jacket, night cap and holsters, rode full speed, as avant courier.

After having spent more than nine months at Paris you will naturally imagine there was a mournful scene of tribulation exhibited in the court of the hotel, the morning of our departure. But really not at all, the sun was blazing so very bright, and challenging so gaily all the world to cheerfulness, that it was impossible not to catch within one's mind the golden tinges which gilded every object. We were going for six months to Italy, and this consideration was a magic talisman, conjuring up so many delirious visions in perspective that hope and expectation bounded forward into futurity, impatiently to forestall the delights of our fluctuating anticipations. . . . There is something ridiculously exhilarating in the cracking of the postillions' whip,

---

* Amelia Opie (1769–1853) née Alderson, wife of John Opie, the painter.
† Stephen, Lord Kilworth, afterwards 3rd Earl Mount Cashell.

as they announce themselves to each town and village, and, as with a look of triumph, they jump out of their preposterous jackboots, which remain empty in the stirrups, till another little fellow bounds upon the saddle and into them, at the same moment, and with the same jerk of activity.

Six hours we drove rapidly on, before we enter'd the beautiful forest of Fontainbleau, and as we look'd through the trees at either side of the road, the sight was lost in its depth and obscurity. The idea of its being the abode of wild boars, wolves, stags etc. together with the darkness suggesting the dread of *banditti*, made me feel not a little pleas'd at entering into the court of the inn, where dinner, coffee, fruits, and welcome greeted us in such profusion that we exchang'd the romance of adventure, with infinite satisfaction, for the vulgar occupation of eating our dinner and going to rest. . . .

Saturday we left Fontainbleau. The French year is at an end and *les cinq jours complementaires* commenc'd on our bidding adieu to Fontainbleau. In Paris this interregnum is fill'd up with fiery fêtes consecrated to Virtue, Genius, Labour, Opinion, and Rewards. The festival of Virtue, we solemniz'd by driving fifty-four miles farther from its commemoration and sleeping at Briare in the *Department l'Yonne*.

Sunday, we drove fifty-two miles on to Nevers in the *Department de la Neive* and after beholding nothing but vineyards for the entire day, reposed our aching eyes in a convent, now transform'd into an inn, where I had the satisfaction of sleeping in the refectory, and seeing the ghosts of departed loaves and fishes.

The church makes excellent stables and as all things end in their commencement, the abolition of religion has placed Christ precisely where He was first created, namely in a manger, which is no more, no less, than a literal fact. For on going into the stable, the first object I saw was the altar piece, exactly as I describe. . . .

The next day we travel'd thirteen posts, and after being pleas'd with a fine extended circle of busy cultivation, at length arriv'd at Roanne, from whence I write, as Lady Mount Cashell's indisposition detains us here some days. The towns I have seen between this and Paris look mouldy and dark, the country looks rich, and the people copper colour'd and degenerating in civilization. . . .

N.B. I am concern'd to garnish the above with a little ornament, indelicately call'd bugs. However to counteract this disgrace, insignificant as Roanne is, it boasts its establishments of baths in which we used to sit for hours, to extirpate the poison which their bite infuses.

Lyons, Department Rhone et Loire. 29 Sept. 1802. 8 Vendemiaire, An. 11. l'Hotel d'Europe, Rue Bonaparte. Place de Belcour.
Another week has elaps'd, which we have spent at this beautiful looking Lyons. The day after I wrote last we quitted Roanne, and in the evening arriv'd here twelve posts. We pass'd la montagne de Farere, which is what I should conceive the scenery of Switzerland to be. The little inn at the foot of this mountain is delightful. The landlord was sitting at a table writing to Bonaparte, and when he had directed his letter *'au premier Consul'*, he took us up to a little bedchamber where, in a transport of pride, he told us that the 'Saviour of his country' had repos'd.

The sign to his inn, was the sun marking its progress on a dial and the motto underneath – '*Ma Revolution est invincible, Telle est la votre François.*' . . .

Nismes, October 6th, 1802. 15me Vendemiaire, An 11. Department du Gard.
This last week has been most delightful. Eight days ago we quitted Lyons and for the first five days sail'd down the Rhone as far as Avignon. Lord Mount Cashell hired a large flat-bottom'd boat, in which the carriages, as well as all our party consisting of fifteen, were excellently accommodated, besides three gentlemen from Lyons. . . . The first day we sail'd seven leagues, and then got on shore to sleep in the village of Condrieux. We

passed the beautiful town of Vienne, where the motion of the boat
shew'd in a hundred different points of view, a most picturesque
looking old cathedral colour'd by time with the tints of an autumn
leaf. The villagers flock'd down to the sides of the boat and threw
in basket-fulls of grapes, at three sous a pound, peaches, pears etc.
in profusion. The wine press is full everywhere, and for the first
time, we saw the process of making wine at Condrieux, where
they gave us *Côte Roti* as it drop'd from the press. In this state, it
tastes very sweet and pleasant. For supper we eat carp, eels, and
pike for which the Rhone is famous. . . .

*Their itinerary seems to have been the one taken by many travellers
going into Italy. Lady Craven just before the Revolution had also sailed
down the Rhône and sampled the Côte-rotie, which she had disliked.*

*The Mount Cashells now continued by river to Avignon, coming
ashore each evening to sleep at the inns on the way, and once, somewhat
frivolously, to run after an air balloon.*

*The scenery through which they were passing varied wonderfully in
its colouring according to the time of day, as though seen, Katherine tells
us, through the differing lenses of a Claude glass. As they went along she
mused on the Romans, Goths, Vandals, who had preceded them, and
listened to the cathedral bell of Viviers echoing among the mountains,
and less pleasurably to Mrs Ruad, the girls' governess, who worked
herself up into a 'rage of sentiment' on the subject of slavery all the way
to Avignon.*

*At Avignon they explored the wonders of the Papal Palace, and would
have gone on to see the famous Fountain of Vaucluse five leagues away,
but left this too for the return journey, 'as every moment must be spared
for crossing the Alps in safety'.*[3]

Before we left Avignon the following day, I went off at six in the
morning in quest of the church in which Petrarch and Laura*
were buried. When we arriv'd at *Les Cordelliers* which is its name,

* Petrarch (Francesco Petrarca) (1304–74), the great Italian poet and romantic, lover of
Laura, a married woman.

I recollected I had seen their tomb at Paris. However, they still point out the arch under which it repos'd for so long a period, and in returning homewards I was attracted by the sight of *Indulgence Plenaire* written over the church door of St Nizier.

It was a fête, and the priests in great solemnity were receiving the sacrament with incense smoking all about them. I observ'd one of the altars whimsically hung about with heads, toes, noses, ears and fingers in wax, but particularly new born infants in miniature, which were strung together like crows' eggs, and hung over the shrine in festoons.

I enquir'd into the history of these irreverent incongruities, and found that miracles had been perform'd at the altar, and that all the women of Avignon who had pass'd the danger of childbirth ascrib'd it to the influence of this shrine, and offer'd a waxen representative of the infant, as a religious trophy.

On returning to the inn, we found all ready for departure and bid adieu to our sailors, who had conducted us safely sixty leagues down the Rhone, with infinite regret, as it was a mode of conveyance by many degrees the most agreeable I ever experienced. . . .

We arriv'd at Nismes and were bit to such an unmerciful degree with bugs, that for my part, I spent the night by the open window finishing my book, being utterly unable to endure the horrors of their persecutions. . . .

Nismes, Department de Gard, 23 Vindemiaire – An 11.
13 Octr. 1802.
We have had enough of time within the last week to examine the curiosities of Nismes. The cause of our making this delay is the division which is to take place in our party. Mrs Ruaud and the two girls, Mr Egan and the three boys, are to stay behind here, while Lord and Lady Mount Cashell, little Richard and I, are to spend the winter in Italy. . . .

19 October – 17 December 1802

Italy, towards which the travellers were now making, was for the most part under French dominion.

Napoleon's Italian campaign of 1796 had been seen by many as a war of liberation against Hapsburg rule in the peninsula, but in 1798 the Austro-Russian armies of the 2nd Coalition counter attacked. Milan and Turin were regained, the young Italian Republics fostered by the French Revolutionary armies collapsed, and everywhere the old order was restored.

Two years later on his return from his Egyptian expedition Napoleon once more engaged with the Austrians, defeating them at Marengo, and French rule was reestablished.

From the traveller's point of view this see-saw of contending armies does not seem to have affected matters all that much. It was certainly noticed how many great works of art were missing in Italian cities owing to pillaging by the French, and some Italians, like the Savoyards, were uncertain where their loyalties lay; there were tales of French brutality. But for the most part Italy seems still to have been the Italy of the great 18th-century Grand Tourists like William Beckford.

Turin, 30me Vendemiaire, An 11. 19th October, 1802.   Rue Neuf.
This last week has presented such a variety of beauty before my eyes that they ache absolutely while I think of all I've seen. But I promise you are to expect no description, for it requires the language of Brobdignag* to convey any conception of the gigantic world, we have been flitting through.

On leaving Nismes in our way towards Grenoble, we spent the two first days in a cold wild desolate country bare and rawboned, rising up perpetually into grim scaldheaded

---

* Brobdignag – the fabulous region in *Gulliver's Travels* where everything was gigantic.

mountains moaning under the prevalence of the north-east wind. . . .

However, the third morning, all the splendour of the weather return'd and with it the magic scenery of Dauphiny which towards Grenoble is uninterruptedly an expanse of garden cover'd with forests of chestnuts and walnut trees, vineyards, cherries, quinzes, pears, medlars, olives, and every species of fruit distributed in the most beautifully abundant manner, over the most diversified country encircled by the Alps. . . .

The fourth night we arriv'd at Montmelian in Savoy, which is in every feature precisely answerable to Switzerland. . . .

I never shall forget the necromantic beauty of one spot where I should have liked to spend my life.* A cave, over which the rock had form'd itself into a gothic castle and mouldering fortifications lost in the shadowings of pine, and symphoniz'd by the music of the waters – the rivulets stealing from their native woods, dimpling through their beds of moss, sparkling with a thousand colours in the sun, foaming over the interlaced branches of the purple flowering heath, and then dashing in diamond-spray from the rocks amongst the dark and beautiful waters of the Isere – the junipers and larch feathering amongst the colour'd clouds and gilt by the sun, which yellow'd into a rock of amber – the transparent snow that crown'd the mountain – everything appear'd more lovely than I can describe!

And this is the spot where my spirit wou'd fain have dwelt, had I not recollected the image of a grim jaw bone that I saw in one of the churches, fram'd in gold and precious stones, which so epitomiz'd the horrid incongruity of myself enshrin'd amidst these wonders, that I turn'd with terror from the thought just on our entry into an inn, happy in a more becoming harbour for such grotesque presumption.

The people of the country are frightful, tho' in their little laced jackets and bordered petticoats, they look picturesque enough

* Here is Katherine the Romantic!

51

in groups at an awful distance. But the guatars* on their throats are terrific, of which they must be perfectly insensible as a defect, for they decorate them with gold trinkets, and look so stupid, that one is sometimes at a loss to find which is the guatar, the face or the throat.

You would have been diverted at seeing us cross the barrier into Piedmont called Mount Cenis. The day before yesterday we left Lansleburg tied on litters like cripples, muzzled, and pack'd in straw, our chairs supported by wild Savoyards. . . .

You cannot conceive anything to compare to the gaiety and wild spirits of our Savoyards, who carried us across the mountain; they went full speed, running races with one another, bounding down the rocks from cliff to cliff, and emulating each other in every feat of activity.

In coming into the little towns, or rather villages, scatter'd on the mountain, they set up a wild song, which brought out all the quatar'd villagers, and after setting us down, like old disabled beggarwomen, at the side of the road, they went in to regale themselves with *vin-du-pays*.

It was quite a part of their trade to amuse us with conversation. Amongst twenty or thirty of them, they severally boasted of being the individual who carried Bonaparte as conqueror out of Italy. But tho' they contested for this honor, they spoke with pleasure of the King of Sardinia,† whom they good humour'dly call'd *roi de marmotes* and seem'd to think the old yoke best. However, they said God was better than either, who gave them sun to ripen yellow their Turkish wheat, and really the effect of it hanging like beads of burnish'd gold against their houses, together with the arbours of yellow flowering gourds, which always shroud their dwellings, adds more than I can express to the contrasted darkness of the boundless forests which crest the splendour of the encircling scene. . . .

Yesterday we had a dreary wet journey of seven posts from

* Goitres.
† Charles Emmanuel iv of Savoy, reigned 1796–1802.

52

Novalese to Turin, and from horrible stories we had heard on the road were in desperate fear of *banditti*. But luckily we met a French regiment which was returning into France, which effectually lull'd our apprehensions. The wives of the officers were all drest, and riding, like men and looking like little boys of fourteen or fifteen years of age.

From Avignon we have experienc'd different gradations of *patois* and even what one hears at Turin, is anything but Italian, nevertheless, they call me Signora for which I am extremely obliged to them, as it is a title that tickles my ear more than I can possibly express.

Turin, 14 Brumaire, An. 11.   Novr. 2nd, 1802 – Rue Neuf.
We have spent a fortnight at Turin, a principal part of which time I was confin'd with a dangerous cold, caught in crossing Mont Cenis. What I have seen, however, you shall hear. . . . However I know how to have compassion on the subject of descriptions of 'Hills and dales, and purling streams' and, therefore, I will pop your imagination for refuge under the little brown wig of Signor Vassali, a Professor of Natural Philosophy, who, together with many others, Lady Mount Cashell got letters of recommendation to, from the Abbé Grégoire.

He is a little old scientific man with the wisdom of centuries and the simplicity of a child, and looks as uninjur'd by time, as if he had been dug out of the ruins of Herculaneum. He has receiv'd great credit for his researches on the subject of Galvanism and one evening brought two or three unfortunate frogs in his pocket, which after having murder'd cruelly, he brought kicking into life again by the application of zinc and silver to the termination of the nerves and muscles.

His mind runs so genuinely on these subjects, that when the French were about the town battering away the fortifications, seizing the citadel, and apprehending traitors, he was groping in a subterraneous passage for bats. Being seen by a French soldier, he was dragg'd before the National Tribunal, charged with plotting against the state and was just going to be escorted to prison, when he took out his snuffy pocket handkerchief in which he had conceal'd his bats, who immediately spread their leathern wings, and flew with such conviction in the face of the judge, that poor Vassali was instantly acquitted, and return'd in triumph amongst his frogs and bats and instruments of natural philosophy. . . .

I won't say anything on the subject of churches, tho' this town contains beautiful ones, because my illness prevented my venturing out at the time they were visited, and indeed I am so reduced that I have no spirits for anything. I believe I should like utter solitude better than any other mode of life. At least I should like the unrestricted power of rolling back into my own existence, like a snail into its shell, without the deplorable necessity of putting out my horns to every intruding blackguard who usurps me from myself.

This you will tell me is *because I did not see the churches*. Wiseacre that you are! make no impertinent reflections upon me, but learn before we quitted Turin we had verified the stories of Italien Revenge, for frequently below stairs the men quarel'd and slash'd at each other with sharp knives on the slightest provocation, nobody daring to interfere or they would indubitably have incurred the same fate.

This I heard from the servants with whom they dined, and whom I envy very often in having a hundred opportunities of familiarizing themselves with the habits and customs of foreign countries, totally denied to their masters and mistresses.

The travellers now proceeded to Milan, entering at Vercelli the Cisalpine Republic formed by Napoleon in 1797 on the model of the Ancient Roman Republic of Transpadana.

At Vercelli the susceptible Lady Mount Cashell formed an enthusiastic friendship (or as Katherine expressed it 'fell victim to') La Signora St Martin La Motte, the charming wife of the Prefect. Churches were visited, they attended the theatre. Concerts, balls, assemblies were projected. When they finally took themselves away the Prefect's secretary kissed Lord Mount Cashell on both cheeks, 'the first time he had

54

undergone the operation', commented Katherine. 'I never was so diverted in all my life as at witnessing the ceremony.'[1]

At Novara they horrifyingly saw a murdered man lying in a ditch, and passed on through teeming rain to Milan. Here, after dinner in their Albergo, a madman appeared, flourishing a pamphlet he had written on the Rights of Women.

Milan fascinated Katherine, the Cathedral especially, where 'mysteriously veil'd before the altar', was a relique set in diamonds and framed in gold and mother of pearl, containing a tooth. Meanwhile in the aisles hovered a ghastly penitent, a 'black Rosary in his wretched thin hand'. He was, Katherine heard to her 'Gothic' satisfaction, a flagrant sinner, and 'the severity of his expiations, had reduced him to this state, and it was feared the hopelessness of absolution would inevitably leave him to perish in the embittering torments of despair . . .'[2]

Florence, 28 Novr. 1802.   8me Frimaire, An 11.   Aquila nera. Albergo Pio.

It is a fortnight since I wrote last. We have since been loitering at Pavia, Plaisance, Parma, Modena, Bologna, and yesterday arriv'd at Florence. . . . Just before we enter'd Pavia, we saw the spot celebrated for the Victory of Charles v over Francis i. On driving into the town, we saw the equestrian statue of Marcus Aurelius Antoninus, the lance of Orlando, etc. and the next day were disabled from going any farther than a few miles by the torrents of rain that fell, and therefore were oblig'd to put up at a miserable wild dismantled looking house, with all the air in the world of being haunted, either with spirits or *banditti.*

Bands of robbers had infested this part of the country, and we heard of the horrid assassination of five men when we were at Milan, which, in an unlucky moment we recollected, must not only have been in this spot, but their murderers harbour'd precisely in this very house, from the description answering so exactly to everything we saw.

On these occasions, whenever Lady Mount Cashell's and my courage began to give way, we consulted the expression of Para's countenance, the courier who knew every inch of the ground, and had served in that publick capacity in the French army during all the campaigns in Italy. He had more address and intrepidity of nature than any man I ever knew; bore hunger, cold and sleeplessness absolutely without the consciousness of their being evils, and, quite with the distinguish'd air of a Cavalier, possess'd a cheerfulness of humour and courtesy of manner, that in the life of adventure we were in, render'd Para a personage of the highest moment.

On our going therefore upstairs, and, from the crack'd panes of the trickling windows, seeing that the rains had swell'd the water so as to moat round the inn like an island, and perceiving everything inside in frightful disorder (the long deal table overturn'd and cut and slash'd with dinner knives upon the surface – a picture of Jesus Christ revers'd upon its peg – and warnings scrawl'd with blood and charcoal against the wall)* we trembled like a pair of arch cowards, and with one accord and at the same moment, ask'd each other what Para thought of the situation we were in.

We instantly went flying in pursuit of him and found him with a parcel of faggots in his arms, coming to light our fire on a flat expanse of hearth, and follow'd by two black hideous looking men, with torn mattresses on their backs, which they flumpt down in a passion in the middle of the floor, and went off growling like a pair of demons.

This did not add much to our composure, nor did Para's face, which was set exactly in that resolute way which augur'd perfect hopelessness on our part of expounding his thoughts, by any questions we cou'd put to him, and therefore we let him follow his inventions, which were these. For the mattresses of straw to be laid round the fire, on which Lady Mount Cashell, the child, and I were to repose cover'd over with our great coats. Candles to burn on the tables throughout the night and the fire to be eternally replenish'd, for which bundles of wood were unwil-

---

* This reads extraordinarily like a Gothic 'phantasy' of Mrs Radcliffe's!

lingly brought into the room. Lord Mount Cashell to be in the little closet within side of us.

For our supper they brought us up a patriarchal cock, with stiff black legs, which seem'd to have died of the gout a month before, and macaroni in a bowl writhing into a hundred serpents. The door was then lock'd and we were to await our doom till morning.

You may imagine the kind of night we spent. The wind was roaring a hurricane, and the rain pattering frightfully against the windows. There were no shutters to prevent our seeing bright blue flashes of lightning fork across the room, or hearing the crashes of thunder breaking in hollow echoes amongst the Apennines, which eternally reminded us of these mountains being the resort of legions of *banditti*, who always find in their recesses a sanctuary from the pursuits of justice.

During the entire night we heard the rumbling of voices underneath, and occasionally cou'd discern Para's in an authoritative tone and then violent bursts of laughter which were again overpower'd by a clap of thunder.

Strange, and most inexplicable as it may appear, after our staying awake breathless with apprehension, heark'ning to every noise we heard, we at length forgot our woes, and were woke by Para's unlocking the door in the clear light of a rising sun.

We at first look'd upbraidingly at one another, for our insensibility. Then felt incredulous at finding ourselves alive, and at length began to recollect our good fortune in having escaped the dangers of the place, from which we made as expeditious a sortie as we possibly cou'd with Para galloping by our sides in high delight.

The moment we were clear off, he rode up to the carriage window and congratulated us on our escape from the most complete cut-throat spot in Italy.

He had arm'd himself with pistols, had given some defensive weapon to William and stillettos to the two *voituriers*, Louis and François, all of whom resolv'd on sitting amongst the people of the inn during the night, round the kitchen fire, drinking and carousing, and cajoling them by a thousand methods.

They let out, he said, in conversation, a hundred things which confirm'd every suspicion of its being, not only a harbour for assassins but of the landlord and his sons being privy to the murders and sharing in the plunder. In short he most thoroughly confirm'd all our apprehensions and made us feel that his address of conduct, together with the accident of its being a market day and the people a good deal about the roads, alone saved us from the fate many have suffer'd in that frightful den of horrors and assassinations. . . .

The fourth night we got to Parma, where we stay'd two days. . . . From Parma to Modena the drive is highly beautiful, the country rich and cover'd with vineyards which are cultivated sometimes by one vine being bent down to the root of another, so as to give the ground the undulating look of a sea running high in a storm, and sometimes they are as high as the forest trees on which they are supported and which they ornament with garlands and festoons in abundance. We cross'd the Tessinaro, over which the Duke of Parma built a bridge, as well as over every other river in his dominions. We stay'd at Modena a day, . . . piously to visit one of the finest cathedrals in Italy, or rather the finest tower, to the top of which we trotted to see the view of the surrounding town. . . .

The next day we drove from Modena to Bologna. . . . We drove full speed about the town in a German barouche, which was a relief after the funereal pace of our *voituriers*. . . . In passing by we saw a church lit up, where masses were singing for the repose of some noble's soul. The entire altar was yellow with candles, and the church elegantly hung in transparent drapery of saffron crape, edg'd and spotted with black velvet – white festoons intermix'd like ermine with black tails, and priests in choirs chanting round the coffin which was erected in the middle on a pyramidical monument, cover'd with gold, and blazing in light.

In the evening we went to the theatre, one of the finest in Italy, built of stone, and more cheerful looking than any I have seen. Banti sang angelically in the opera of *Oedipus*. The company was numerous, and look'd pretty much like a Parisian assemblage, excepting that the ladies were not so classically dress'd. . . .

As to the famous sausages of Bologna, we got none, tho' they gave excellent Parmazan cheese, which latter they did not let appear at Parma, but treated us with very fine Bologna sausages!

The next morning we left Bologna, in a melancholy fall of rain and began to ascend the Apennines, in which mountains we were imprisoned for three long days.

During this time our carriages were toss'd about like ships in a storm, such was the rocking, and such the dreadful fatigue. Our accommodations amongst the mountaineers were not much calculated to assuage these effects, as they generally consisted of a hard mattress and stiff short quilt, which let the air blow in in every direction. For eating it did not signify, as we always could get fresh eggs, tho' nothing else, excepting a sort of soup or infamous macaroni.

We were delay'd at *la douane* by the examination of trunks, on passing from the 'Cisalpine Republick'* into Etruria and were stop't so long, that we were compleatly benighted amongst such a collection of black gigantic mountains, that it was impossible to discern them from the heavy clouds of thunder that hung in darkness over our heads.

These frightful Apennines, where bands of assassins to the amount of forty, issue forth sometimes upon unfortunate travellers, and often let stillettos reach their lives! This was no matter of mere apprehension with us, for we had in the morning met nine men in chains escorted towards Milan, for the perpetration of a horrid robbery and murder.

The night was so dark, and the tempest so wild – the floods roaring in the valleys – and the precipices so perpendicular, that

* Napoleon had created the Cisalpine Republic in 1796. Tuscany had been renamed Etruria in 1801.

I don't comprehend how we escaped being blown headlong over the edge of the slippery road which was without an inch of parapet.

In the midst of our danger, the lamps of the carriage were extinguished, and we were left in utter darkness, with the fear of stillettos before our eyes and the horror of desperadoes haunting our imaginations. In the midst of this forlorn plight, we were more appall'd than I can express, at a sudden burst of fire from the top of a distant mountain which yellow'd the black horizon, and for a moment we imagined ourselves the destined victims of an earthquake. But we were consol'd by the muleteers on hearing it was only the eruption of a volcano, which during a storm increas'd so considerably, that the effect became tremendous. Through its means however we discovered a cottage, where we got guides, who conducted us with torches for three miles safely to our journey's end. . . .

Florence, 17 Decr. 1802. 'Aquila Nera', Albergo Pio.
It is three weeks since we arriv'd at Florence, and have prosper'd under the influence of Saint Jean, *patron de la ville.*

'Tis grievous there should be such rivalry in the holy calendar of saints, and that our poor Irish St Swithin cannot be allow'd to enjoy his rainy prerogative in quiet upon the Hibernian shores, without his cannoniz'd brother Jean snatching the watering pot out of his hand, and for one and twenty days almost incessantly sprinkling over this beautiful town without mercy.

We have nevertheless been driving about the streets amongst Venus's, Apollos, Ganymedes, flying Mercurys, Hercules's, Ledas, Wrestlers, Bacchus's, Phaedons, Muses, Nereides, Minervas, so that we have almost forgot we were not among the merry retinue of Jove, and in his feather'd heaven!

These statues, which are of the most exquisite workmanship, seem to start before one into life at every turn and well deserve the honors of a separate collection, but that their value is so well known, that the slightest injury is never offer'd to them, even through the mischief of playful children.

Florence seems to me to be made entirely of different colour'd marbles. All the churches are of black and white, and the Cathedral does not look unlike an Indian tea chest of inlaid ebony and ivory, on a prodigious scale. The streets too are paved with marble, and everything almost monumental of the house of Medici. The gallery of paintings founded by them five hundred years ago, has suffer'd sadly by the pillage of the French. We have visited it frequently, and every day return'd home, more and more delighted at the hope of returning there again. . . .

'Tis melancholy to see the famous octagonal chamber call'd the Tribuna with its five empty pedestals. What once fill'd them we saw at Paris, except the Venus de Medici which had not arriv'd from Palermo. But God knows Venuses of one sort or other are so abundant in these galleries, that 'tis absolutely impossible to believe the number can be added to or, in many instances, the beauty made superior. . . .

Monsignore Morozzo, the Pope's Nuncio, call'd in the evening. He announced himself on his ticket 'Archevèque de Thebes, Nonce Apostolique pres S: M: le Roi d'Etruier', and suddenly a tall, thin, transparent looking man in black silk robes, gold chain, scarlet callote and purple stockings flitted in a hundred bows before our eyes. He appear'd full of Papal profundity and aristocratical gossip, and open'd the party schism of the town by piously informing us, no salvation was to be found out of the Noble Pale. Superstition and bigotry hold their court in the souls of the ignorant and consequently this man's sway is omnipotent amongst the Florentine nobility.

After he disappear'd the Princess Montimoletto, a Neapolitan, accompanied by Signor Tassoni, the Minister of the Italian Republick, came to take us to the theatre. . . . La nobil Donna, la Signora Marchese Santini, a fat wicked looking woman, crown'd with red roses, came to take us next evening to Madame la Comtesse d'Albani, widow to the Pretender,* grandson of James II.

---

* Charles Edward Stuart (1720–88), 'Bonny Prince Charlie'.

61

She was born in the low countries, and after being affianced by her father to the Pretender, she was oblig'd to live with him some time. But circumstances deranging his conduct, she gain'd a divorce through the Grand Duke of Tuscany, Leopold. The Count Alfier* had always been Madame Albani's *cavaliere servente*,† and suspicions attaching to him as the cause of her separation from the Count,‡ he was banish'd accordingly. Since the death of her husband he has reassum'd this post, and always lives in the same house with her.

He is call'd the Shakespeare of Italy and we met him at her *conversaziones* to which he did not much contribute, for tho' so great a tragic hero, he dwindles into nothing in society, which he only looks at like a picture, while for hours he stands leaning on the mantel-piece, without ever unsealing his lips to mortal. This evil is trifling, if his august presence did not cast an intolerable damp upon the rest of the company.

Every thursday we have frequented this house. They play chess, sometimes cards, give tea *à l'Anglaise*, and spend the chief time in conversation. As the latter is professedly the object of the evening, everybody appears rather performing a duty than relaxing in amusement and often restraint is the inevitable consequence. . . .

We have been at two balls given by la Marchese Torrigiani, a very elegant little creature. Her boudoir was lit by one of the alabaster antique lamps, suspended in the middle of the room by chains, and throwing the softest light through its own transparency. The ceiling was form'd in a dome, stain'd blue, and spangled with gold stars, and a beautiful piece of clockwork representing Apollo with his lyre, told the hour by a musical chime, whenever a particular spring was touch'd.

It was as large as life, and I can't describe to you the beauty of the effect. The chairs, like those in Paris, were all in different shapes and patterns copied from the antique, and just such as

* Vittorio, Count Alfieri (1749–1803), Italian dramatic poet.
† Gallant.   ‡ The Pretender.

one sees in the picture of Cornelia exhibiting the Gracchi or such sort of representations. I became acquainted in a dancing way, with the Prince Corsini, who is one of the most gentlemen-like young men I ever saw, and his brother who, on the strength of the Prince's acquaintance, came up and talk'd to me the next evening, reminds me of an anecdote which I heard from twenty people that night.

He is a *cavaliere servente* to La Bentivoglia, a sad virago of a woman, who not pleased with some conduct of his, which rather excited her indignation, fell upon him and literally gave the poor Prince as sound a beating as he ever got in his life. I don't suppose this is a common prerogative, or else it would not have been so much talk'd of. However such things are, and the Prince and she had arranged matters so happily that, tho' a separation was talked of, all now is brought to an accommodation. . . .

I'll say no more about society, as we shall return here the latter end of April, to stay a longer time than we have been able to do at present. But of the point which renders society less pleasant to strangers, at least than it otherwise would be, I must say a word because I understand tho' the custom of *cicisbeoism* exists all over Italy, it does not produce such disagreeable effects anywhere as at Florence.

The tenacity of the beautiful Florentine for a numerous retinue of admirers, makes her feel so apprehensive of a rival, that she is evidently unhappy when anyone draws the observation of her lovers from immediate attention to herself. The degrees of these admirers are mark'd by the gradations which the following terms announce. First, the favourite who is the *cicisbeo*, then the *ganzo*, then the *aspirante*, who hopes to supply the place of the cashiered one and he again at a more humble distance is call'd *patico*. This applies only to ladies of the highest rank, for altho' the system is universal, those in inferior situations have not more than one gentleman attendant. In numerous instances these *cicisbeos* may be call'd lovers, in many others guardians, and in others I have remark'd, mere servants, to run about on messages, carry the lady's shawl on his arm, and conduct her from one house to another.

Husbands and wives however fond they may be of one another, are never seen together out of their own house. This I observ'd in various instances, where the affection was unfeign'd in both parties. All these practices disgust a person of any delicacy or correctness. . . .

I will now release you from this long sojournment at Florence, tho' I have said nothing of its surrounding Apennines, of its fine cypresses, of its Cascina,* of its beautifully flowing Arno, or in short of what will be better seen in summer, tho' of rains I have complain'd not without reason. Yet there is a satin softness in the air beyond anything I ever felt anywhere at the other side the Alps, and every morning at breakfast the room is strewn over with baskets of roses, orange blossoms, carnations, mignonette, and flowering myrtle, brought to be sold by the peasant girls in gold brocaded petticoats, scarlet stockings, real pearl earrings and necklaces of an immense size, and braided hair interwoven with colour'd cords, and bunches of flowers. In this dress they walk in processions and make offerings to the Holy Virgin.

* Public park.

1 January – 6 March 1803

The Mount Cashells now left for Naples, making brief halts at Siena, Viterbo and at Rome for Christmas, where they could hardly see through the thick mist enveloping the city.

Intending to return in April for Holy Week, they stayed just long enough to admire St Peter's, and among other sights, visit the Villa Borghese.

Here before their eyes danced a succession of 'Fighting Gladiators, Cupid and Psyche, Egyptian Idols, Satyrs, Centaurs, Sphinxes, Graces, Bacchanals, Narcissuses, Venuses, Sarcophagi, Roman Emperors . . . Vases, Idols, Crocodiles, Ganymedes . . .'[1]

Then on, via Veletri, Terracina and along the Appian Way to Capua, and eventually to Naples itself.

The Bourbon kingdom of Naples had suffered particularly as a consequence of the French Revolutionary wars.

French Republican influence had finally precipitated civil war in the kingdom between the reactionary king (his queen was the sister of Marie Antoinette) and his devoted following of the commonalty – the 'lazzaroni' – and the aristocracy, who favoured a moderate Republicanism.

The phases of this civil war in which Britain and her allies perforce supported the king, were marked by appalling atrocities, and finally resulted in a Royalist victory.

When the king returned from Palermo where he had fled with his court in Nelson's ships, a truly Neapolitan revenge was exacted from the Republicans. The worst example was the treacherous execution without trial of Baron Caracciolo, the Republican admiral, on the deck of Nelson's ship.

By the time the Mount Cashells and Katherine arrived in Naples however all was quiet again, though not forgotten.

65

January 1st, 1803.   Naples, Aquila Nera.
. . . It being the 1st of January 1803, we made our entry into Naples where everything look'd like a new world.

The paintings of hell, heaven, and purgatory flaming everywhere against the walls – little carriages of a thousand colours looking like china flower pots calculated to hold but one person, driving like wildfire about the streets – heavier and more magnificent equipages drawn in gay procession, the horses ornamented with bunches of artificial flowers, and knots of ribbon – groups of *lazzaroni* lapping slow their macaroni – monks and Capuchins in endless lines of expiatory dirges – crucifixions, holy emblems, Christmas symbols – Improvisatores haranging their incircling mob. In short, eternally diversified objects changing before our eyes, as we drove through the town. Till on turning round towards the Corso on the sea shore, the beautiful Bay of Naples thirty miles in circumference, and twelve in diameter open'd upon us in dazzling splendour, and more than justified all our expectations.

Thousands of little painted barks, with their prows gilt and gayly flower'd, lay glittering on the strand, and as many more danc'd upon the waves, and look'd like everything one's fancy coin'd of nereides, scaly dolphins, and magic shells, which once were common in this fabled land.

Naples, March 6th, 1803.
We have spent nine weeks in this enchanting land and so much of pleasure and entertainment has been mingled throughout this period, that if I cou'd transfer to your mind the general impression I have experienced of all that gave me amusement, I believe you wou'd imagine we had been here a twelvemonth, from the variety of ideas that lie scatter'd within my fancy.

But really and truly, such has been the rapidity with which burning mountains, kings and queens, masquerades, Herculaneums, improvisatories, tombs of Virgil, grotta del canes, Salfaterras, balls, churches, fortresses, coasts of Baia, princes and princesses, Monte-Nouvas, *cicisbeos*, mountebanks,

66

nuns, theatres, Capuchins, catacombs, miracles, and all sorts of incongruities have cross'd my brain that literally I might as well attempt to methodize a mob, as to organize the ingredients which run foul of one another in my memory.*

This much I recollect, that for the first week I stood at the window gazing at Mount Vesuvius which is before our eyes, at the opposite side of the Bay, looking like a sugar loaf with the pinnacle broke off and smoking from the mouth of the chasm. The view from the balcony was so beautiful that every morning, as I stood there, really and truly the loveliness of the scene deluded me into every species of credulity. . . .

The twelfth of Jan. there was a grand presentation at court, where the King and Queen receiv'd all the English, who were introduc'd by their Minister, Mr Drummond,[†] immediately after the royal dinner at half past twelve o'clock.

During the repast they all stood by and had the honor of beholding the King and Queen, Prince hereditary and his Spanish bride, cramming like dragons and lapping their choco-late cream for the edification of their loving subjects, who throng'd in admiration about their chairs.

Lord Mount Cashell was the only one of us who went. He like all the other gentlemen was dress'd in velvet and embroidery, ruffles, bag and sword. The Queen and Princess were in hoops, long waists, diamond stomagers [sic] and lappets. The former a wicked politician and far from possessing the elegance which one might expect from the sister of Marie Antoinette. The latter, a little girl of fifteen years of age, as round as an apple, and, without knowing how to read or write or speak anything but Spanish, resists every means of instruction offer'd her by the Queen and is perfectly contented in the prospect of reigning some day over Naples.

---

* The use of impressionistic lists of this sort probably began with Horace Walpole – 'precipices, mountains, torrents, wolves, rumblings, Salvator Rosa . . .' he wrote of the Alps.

† Sir William Drummond (1770–1820), afterwards Ambassador to Turkey.

This being the King's birthday, it was an universal gala, and in the evening all the world went to the theatre of St Carlos, which is reckon'd the most beautiful one in the world. We went to the Princess Charace's box, in which were the two reigning belles of Naples, her daughter the Princess di Cassano Aragona, and her daughter-in-law the Duchess of Terranova, both uncommonly pretty women. A succession of brocaded Princes during the entire evening frequented the box, dress'd in cut velvet embroider'd suits, swords and bags, etc.

The display of diamonds among the ladies surpassed everything I cou'd have imagin'd, everyone blazed like a constellation! The seams of their gowns even were studded with diamonds, and what with diamond chains, necklaces, sprays of brilliants, towering on the head like feathers, diamond nets, combs, head-dresses, and fringes to the gowns etc., really our eyes ached at looking at all we saw. Everyone was the same, and my fancy would have made me believe myself in the country of Golconda,* had I not been inform'd that amongst the nobility, all the women were Princesses or Duchesses, and that if twenty daughters were in a family, all the accomplishments, money and diamonds are given to one, and the rest shut up in convents for life. These convents abound here, as well as everywhere else in Italy.

During the night, a profusion of cakes and ices were handed about in the box. This is the fashion in Naples, and in many boxes, cold suppers of hams, pies, macaroni etc. Scarcely any attention was paid to the performance excepting when the principal vocal musick began, and then they deign'd to look sometimes on the stage and were moved to the most animated expressions of delight. As during the time we were at Naples we went for an hour almost every evening to this or one of the other theatres, I observ'd very frequently the curtains of the boxes scarcely undrawn and, but that we heard voices, and saw their

---

* The ancient name for Hyderabad – a synonym for wealth.

moving shadows, we should have been totally unconscious whether they were inhabited or not.

I liked exceedingly the fashion of paying visits about the house, instead of getting the cramp from the stagnation of an entire night. You are conducted about by a gallant *cavalliere*, first to one box, then to another, upstairs and down stairs, until you come puffing and blowing back again to the box you left, where you find in general quite a fresh assortment of company from those you had quitted. . . .

The profound allegiance of *cicisbeoism* is not observ'd here by any means, as at Florence. On the contrary 'tis difficult to perceive it exists from the community of gay good-fellowship reigning throughout society, with an utter extinction of either that reserve or jealousy, so observable elsewhere, and so distructive to the spirit of society. Nevertheless the system is precisely the same and, strange to say, the Italian husbands absolutely despise their wives, if through any neglect of those accomplishments which attract admirers, they disqualify themselves from possessing the usual complement of surrounding satellites. . . .

The Portuguese Minister and his beautiful wife, Madame Sa, who was his grand niece, are very principal in making us pleasant in Naples. We dined at a most splendid entertainment given by him to all the ambassadors at half past two o'clock, where we met swarms of velvet coats, bags and swords, and after dinner went to the palace where Mr Drummond, in all due form, presented Lady Mount Cashell and me to her Majesty the Queen of Naples.

The audience was not above ten minutes, and then we drove off to the Minister Acton's* ball, where we met the King, Queen, hereditary Prince and Princess, and all the royal household. On

* Sir John Acton, 6th Baronet (1736–1811), Prime Minister of Naples. Son of Edward Acton, a physician at Besançon, he served in the Tuscan navy in a joint expedition with Spain against Algiers and was thereafter rapidly promoted at the Court of Naples.

their entrance, all their liege subjects fell on one knee and kiss'd their hands and nobody sat in their presence.

The Queen is a sturdy looking dame by no means elegant in her deportment, and trotted about in her black and blue robes, much more as if she was crying 'tooky, tooky, tooky!' after her poultry, like a housewife, than a Queen doing the dignities of her drawing room.

The King looks like an overgrown ass, tho' in his demeanour he is exceeding civil. However, his face surpasses any abridgement of imbecility I ever saw in all my life, and the vulgar debauchée reigns triumphant throughout his Majestic exterior.

The hereditary Prince delights in dancing which he does like a cow cantering. Vulgar is no expression to apply to his appearance, for vulgarity becomes genteel within his presence. He danced with his little Spanish bride, and when he is at the bottom of a set, he walks her up to the top again, and sets off kicking up his hoofs, and making a sort of noise like the braying of an ass. His sisters are prettyish, thin and light hair'd, and glittering like all the court in diamonds. The multitudes of fine dress'd people and splendour of the rooms made it exceedingly entertaining, tho' it did not tend much to establish the divine right of monarchs, in any other way then shewing their dissimilarity from any mortals I ever saw before in all my life . . . before I speak more of the society of Naples, which is as dull to talk of, as agreeable to partake of, I will tell you of an expedition I made to Mount Vesuvius.

We drove from Naples to Herculaneum, where we mounted mules and with guides rode up to the hermitage call'd il Salvatore where, after taking a little repast with the hermit, we mounted our mules again, and proceeded about half way up the mountain, where we were oblig'd to alight, and by the means of cords fastened round the waists of our guides which we held, were pull'd heavily up to the top of the mountain more dead than alive after the exertion.

From Herculaneum to above the hermit's cells, the lava, over which we rode, had the appearance of dirty melted iron reduced to cinders and was all loose crumbling dross and ashes in which we plunged half way up our legs, and these materials giving way under our feet, we slid back almost every step we went, till our guides, with the help of staffs fork'd with iron stay'd their hold, and so advanc'd us after them by degrees. By the time I got to the top, my foot was bleeding through my boot, tho' I had on a pair of strong ones, made for the occasion.

The view this eminence commands is really charming of all the principal objects of the town, shore, Bay, coast of Baia, etc. We held a council of war, and it was agreed the ladies, who were Mrs Derby, a beautiful little American, and myself, should sit contemplating the view, while the gentlemen descended into the crater. However, we were suddenly fired with a spirit of enterprise, and resolv'd on going too, which we accomplish'd at the peril of our lives. For we were obliged to totter round the edge of the gulph on this crumbling cindery soil, which was so shallow that one cou'd scarcely walk, and the frightful depth of the crater to the left, and the steep side of the mountain to the right really render'd it perilous beyond description. Mrs Derby kneel'd down, shut her eyes, and had herself trail'd along as well as she cou'd. My head got giddy and I thought I should have fainted with fright. However the deed was to be done, and committing myself to the conduct of three guides who hook'd my arm upon a pole, and dragg'd me along, I also shut my eyes, and at length got to the spot where we descended into the crater.

The same loose slaty sort of cinders were to be waded through till we got to the bottom. The general appearance of the surface was dark green and yellowish from the quantities of smoking sulphur and so broken into waves that it look'd like the sea in storm, suddenly congeal'd. The fissures in the sides of the mountain emitted a curly white smoke, which issuing from all parts intercepted the atmosphere, and made us feel the heat suffocating, so that we did not spend above half an hour at the bottom. However whether an eruption was to have sent us flying up into the air like rockets or a fiery gulph of boiling lava to have open'd under our feet, it did not signify, for we were

71

obliged to rest after our fatigues, and the way Mrs Derby employ'd herself was writing a little letter to her friends in America, descriptive of the surrounding scenery.

The extent we contemplated all around us of angry volcanic substance wrench'd into shapeless masses, some day to burst up into a shower of death as formerly on Pompeia and Herculaneum gave such a wild chaotic guise to all we saw, that nothing could more properly substantiate the picture of Milton's Pandemonium than the scene of which we form'd our ornamental part, smoked as we were like demons, 'prone on the ground extended long and large and floating many a rood'.

In many places the heat was insupportable to the touch and when again we found ourselves on the top of the volcano, the scene had varied into starlight beauty, which little required the contrast it received by rising as we did grim out of the bowels of the earth. The Bay expanded in a wider circumference and look'd like a sheet of mother of pearl studded throughout with its lovely islands, circled by its orange wooded shores . . .

All this time our poor dear long-ear'd mules were waiting either with Christian or Mythologic patience tramping the hollow mountain, and tumbling great masses rattling to its base, which seem'd descending down a mile from the return of their echoes.

We trotted down almost as rapidly as the stones fell, retraced our roads of lava, pumice, and vitrification, and return'd to Herculaneum, or rather Portici, where the carriages were waiting in which we drove full speed back again to Naples. . . .

We spent a delightful day at le Citoyen Alquier's, l'Ambassador de la Republique Française, where was all the foreign diplomacy. These entertainments here resemble those I have describ'd to you of the Parisian ones, so that it wou'd be only repetition to talk to you of the lingering *conversaziones*, which in fact they are, extended to the length of two or three hours, the inversion of solids and whipt-sillibubs, the ladies and gentlemen leaving the room together, the coffee and liqueurs etc. But what I did not see in France and what I believe is only seen in perfection in Italy, is a nun taking the veil, which we witness'd twice since we were at Naples.

The ceremony I am going to mention occurr'd in consequence of the fix'd intention a young lady had taken, absolutely contrary to the wishes, prayers and entreaties of her entire family to renounce the world and dedicate a blooming life to the worship of the saints.

We accompanied her aunt, the Duchess of Campochiara, the night previous to the grand and final ceremony, to the convent, where all her relations and friends to the number of two hundred, dress'd in courtly gear were assembled waiting for her performance of these first religious rites, which qualified her entrance into an everlasting tomb.

She at length appear'd dazzling in diamonds, with her hands folded across her breast, and her eyes cast upon the ground, hung over like a victim with flowery garlands, and slowly walking through the crowd who open'd a passage for her, as she silently mov'd towards the convent gate, where she flung herself on her knees, and knock'd against the door for admittance. . . .

Instantly the wide folding gates flew open, and there appear'd the black veil'd sisterhood, but principally the Abbess, who received her in her arms, symbolical of the Church of Christ.

Everyone then, one by one, walk'd up the steps, not daring to overstep the sacred threshold, and, embracing the lovely novice, congratulated her on the approaching sacrifice. This ended the evening ceremony.

The next morning we return'd to the church belonging to the convent she was about to enter. On stopping at the gate, three or four young men in court dresses came to meet us, and putting our hands under their arms, led us up the aisle, and seated us almost before the altar, where priests were officiating, and where the most sweet and solemn musick echo'd throughout the vaulted roofs in expiatory peals. . . .

The hymns were appropriate for the occasion – the church appear'd almost made of lapis lazuli and stain'd glass – the frankincense perfum'd all around, and such was the effect which insensibly stole upon everyone's imagination, that when like a saint she appear'd at the grating, usher'd by triumphal choirs of priests, not only the women, but many of the young Englishmen were in indignant tears. One, just by me, instinctively lay'd his hand upon his sword, swearing that such heartrending superstitious cruelties ought to be extirpated from off the face of the earth.

All was in a moment silent as death, and everyone was obliged to see, and everyone obliged to hear the snapping of the scissors, which separated a hundred glossy braids and curls from her head, which fell amongst her bands of roses at the feet of the Abbess, who continued with unrelenting piety to strip her of every ornament, and then bound her temples with sack-cloth and threw over her the black austerities of her holy order, placing a crown of thorns upon her head, a branch of white lilies in her hand, a large crucifix by her side, and all the insignia of a heavenly office. She then disappear'd amongst a black procession of deep veil'd nuns, each with lighted torches in their hands, preceded by the elevation of the host.

This that takes up two minutes to relate, took four hours to witness. The musick was so supremely delightful, the processions so numerous, the masses so eternal, and the exhortations so endless, that I felt as if I had spent a little life amongst the cloisters, and as nothing but my imagination was engag'd, it was totally a new existence, breaking from the delusions of the church, into the dazzling blear of day. . . .

The weather has been most gloriously fine and we have made various expeditions about the country within the last month. Among the rest we drove under the Grotto of Posilippo, a couple of miles out of town to the Grotto del Cane on the borders of the Lago d'Agnano, and saw the effects of the carbonic acid gas on a dog, whose mouth was held down to the bottom of the cave, where after inhaling it half a minute he became apparently dead, but recovered instantly in the atmospheric air. A pistol was fired off in it without any report, a torch extinguished and all the usual experiments duly made. . . . Mr Burdett, Sir Francis's brother, is eternally of our parties, a young man exceedingly fond of improvement, and highly amiable. We all went to visit the catacombs.

At the present day these catacombs are full of skeletons, and inclosures for the dead are made at either side of the wall. Various miracles are wrought amongst these raw heads and bloody bones, particularly at the tomb of a saint, whose blood we were constrain'd to confess to our guide was still liquid on the ground, tho' with my natural eyes I cou'd discern nothing but dust and stones.

Attach'd to this grim and endless repository for the dead, through which we walk'd with flambeaux smoking in our faces, is a convent of a poor establishment. We walk'd all through it. The nuns were dress'd in stone blue cloth jackets and petticoats with puff'd cloth sleeves, and forehead binders of white linen. They appear'd more anxious for the flesh than the spirit, for their occupation was throughout the entire convent, nothing scarcely but cooking their dinners, which they perform'd separately in a little crucible of a pot, over a brazier, and excepting that I saw a few lean spare figures kneeling in the middle of the rooms, and telling their beads before a crucifix, I should have been unconscious I was not in a house of industry, or amongst a group of manufacturers. . . .

The sight-seeing continued relentlessly. Pompei, 'most interesting of all places',[2] where Katherine, as tourists still do, gazed fascinated at the traces of the carriage wheels, the soldiers' graffiti, the rooms in the houses painted in mythological stories, 'their colours as vivid as the freshest flowers'[3] not to mention the impressive public buildings.

By comparison Herculaneum, where they descended into the bowels of the earth with flaming torches to look for the town, was something of a disappointment, though her quick mind enjoyed the miraculous transition from the ruins to the Carnival of modern Naples – 'a lapse of 17 Centuries'.

Here the masks were riding about in their open carriages, in every sort of ridiculous character, bombarding each other with sugar comfits.

Lake Avernus and the Baths of Nero, the tomb of Scipio Africanus, the Castle of Baia – much as they thrilled her, she found herself regretting her lack of classical knowledge, and wishing that her brother, Robert, trained as he was in the classics could have changed places with her . . .

I forgot to mention Saint Januarius, the patron of this place, tho' fallen considerably since the horrors of the French. His blood has fail'd to liquify, and he has incurr'd the heavy and obstreperous indignation of the Neapolitans, who never fail to remind him of his obligations, and abuse him in the most outrageous manner, for the suspension of the miracle.

This however is a sore subject, as it is combined with the remembrances of a period too recent to be spoken of even in general terms, as there is scarcely any one that one sees who is not a living victim to its cruelties from a brother, father, son, or near relation having fallen in the cause.

The conduct of Lady Hamilton is universally consider'd, not only as a slur upon her sex and country, but upon humanity. To her influence over the weak mind of Lord Nelson, the breach of treaties, as well as individual persecution, is attributable. During the execution of Caracciolo* and his own [Nelson's] physician who saved his life, Cherillo, and others of the revolution on board his ship, which tinged the Bay with blood, Lady Hamilton sat contemplating on deck the detail'd miseries of the wretched sufferers, reclining upon a chair and affecting the theatrical display of grief by a white pocket handkerchief which she had waving in the air, and changing into the most graceful attitudes.

This circumstance together with a hundred others, I heard repeated by dozens of eye-witnesses. But here I'll stop! for to convey any idea of all that pass'd, would be wading through such a sea of blood, that it would be horrible and now useless to recapitulate it!

* Prince Francesco Caracciolo (1732–99), Neapolitan admiral and Republican.

76

17 April – 10 July 1803

On 6 March they unwillingly prised themselves away from Naples, having already planned to be back at Rome in time for Holy Week.

When they reached their hotel in the suffocatingly 'English' colony of Place d'Espagne, they were still mourning Naples. Then, as Katherine expressed it, they pulled themselves together and 'seriously set about our examination of everything that was to be seen above and under ground . . .'[1] in Rome. But she was to find that Rome swarmed both above and underground with such endless curiosities 'that I now break from the task with desperation . . .'[2]

April 17th, 1803. Rome. Place d'Espagne, Hotel Pio.

You may imagine us for hours together rooting like moles in the bowels of the earth, or visiting thousands of palaces full of fine paintings, or walking through galleries of sculptured gods, goddesses, heroes and heroines. In short, since the creation of Rome to the present day, as far as vestiges can represent reality, you may fancy us each minute passing from century to century, from Paganism to Christianity, from Jupiters to Crucifixions, from Heros to Saints, from Rhea's Sylvias to Virgin Marys, from Pantheons to Vaticans, and so on, in such perpetual succession that you will begin to forget that I too am not cut out of a block of marble.

So much of sculpture have I passed through, and so much of admiration have I experienced that, if wonder had any petrifying powers, I might long since have turn'd into stone. Indeed I suspect this metamorphosis did take place, and but for a visit I paid to Angelique Kauffman,* I might have remain'd so till doomsday, but her promethean influence which animates

---

* Angelica Kauffman (1742–1807), a Swiss artist, who settled in London.

77

everything she touches, tingled me into existence once again, nor can I think of her without a flash of admiration such as her nature is calculated to inspire, independent of the talent which has rendered her name so celebrated.

She allows us to sit with her often in the mornings, as her delicate state of health makes confinement necessary. Her appearance has so much more of mind than body, that one forgets she is more than half way past to another world, which seems anticipated in her countenance, tho' view'd through so much fancy that genius counteracts her piety and in advance she sees a mythologic heaven reflected in her imagination.

Her delightful mildness of manners and sweetness of voice soothes one like the effect of plaintive musick, and the pale transparency of her complexion, one attributes less to her declining health, than to the idea that no other light has ever shone on her, but the silver beams of the moon.

She speaks when you like of her profession, but it is so secondary an object in one's visit to her house, that we forgot to ask for her pictures till the third time we were in her company. She still continues painting, tho' but slowly, and she seems highly consider'd amongst modern artists. One of her pictures of the latest invention, is *The Parting of Coriolanus and his Family*, which is extremely beautiful in the design as well as in the execution. However, in general, portraits are what occupy her pencil, and more her pencil than her genius.

Lord Bristol,* the Bishop of Derry, lives in her neighbourhood. As his house is an exhibition of the fine arts, we went to see it, and were amused as well with its contents, as the singularity of the arrangement. He is the patron of all modern artists, whose wives he not only associates with as his only female company, but has their pictures drawn as Venuses all over the house. His three favourite mistresses are beautifully represented as Juno, Minerva and Venus, in *The Judgment of Paris*.

* Frederick Augustus, 4th Earl of Bristol and Bishop of Derry (1730–1803).

Tho' he is one of the greatest curiosities alive, yet such is his notorious character for profane conversation and so great a reprobate is he in the most unlicensed sense of the word, that the English do not esteem it a very creditable thing to be much in his society, excepting only where curiosity particularly prompts. I have often seen him riding and driving past our windows and his appearance is so very singular that I must describe it to you.

His figure is little, and his face very sharp and wicked. On his head he wore a purple velvet night cap, with a tassel of gold dangling over his shoulder and a sort of mitre to the front, silk stockings and slippers of the same colour, and a short round petticoat, such as bishops wear, fringed with gold about his knees. A loose dressing gown of silk was then thrown over his shoulders. In this merry andrew trim he rode on horseback to the never-ending amazement of all beholders!

The last time I saw him, he was sitting in his carriage between two Italian women, dress'd in white bed-gown and night cap like a witch, and giving himself the airs of an Adonis. The stories one hears of him are endless, both in the line of immorality and irreligion, and in general he contrives to affront everyone he invites to his table. To counterbalance all this, he admires the arts, supports the artists, and spends such a quantity of money in Italy, that amongst other rarities which he has purchased, he has also purchased friends. However, his residence at Rome has thoroughly confirm'd the idea which most foreigners have of the English character being the most bizarre in the world, bizarre but generous. . . .

One of our first expeditions from Rome was to Frascati, now particularly distinguish'd as the residence of the Cardinal Duke of York,* brother to the Pretender. We were presented to him by Cardinal Erskine, and spent a singularly entertaining day.

He is about seventy-eight years of age, still uncommonly handsome, with the freshness of youth in his cheeks, tho' unable to walk without support. He holds his court with as

---

* Henry, Cardinal York (1725–1807), last of the Stuarts.

much regal etiquette as possible, and everybody calls him 'Your Royal Highness' when they address him, which is an observance he exacts, being tenacious of the fading shadow of royalty which he believes his legal right.

His residence is very pretty, in the midst of lovely gardens, where he walks as much and as often as he can and performs his religious duties sometimes in an arbour. He was so employ'd, after our presentation, while we were driving about in his carriage which was ready at the door to conduct us through the neighbourhood.

We drove to the beautiful Villa Aldobrandini, belonging to the Prince Borghese . . . Aldobrandini is famous for its water-works which rise out of the ground at a touch, to the amazement sometimes of those who see them playing all round them, without the power of extricating themselves. Music too breaks from the surrounding gods and goddesses sculptured round the place and produces a pretty effect.

After seeing pictures, palaces, and so forth, we return'd at two o'clock to dinner with the Cardinal Duke of York. There were no ladies, except ourselves, so he placed Lady Mount Cashell on one side, and me on the other, and the rest of the company consisted of cardinals, bishops, and one Capuchin.

He had a plate, napkin, salt-seller, and glass, different from the others, and nobody eat till after he was help'd. Except for this, he was free from ceremony and pleased with the conviviality which reign'd around. After going upstairs to the drawing room, we were shewn by Cardinal Locatelli, the chalice, mitre etc. set in diamonds, emeralds and rubies, all appertaining to the Duke's chapel which was beautifully fitted up. They all then sat down to cards and we were taken to the top of the house to admire the prospect. Afterwards Lady Mount Cashell was presented with a medal engraved with a strong likeness of the Cardinal, and 'Henry ix' written on the other side.

The blithesome gaiety of this pious conclave of holy men was very pleasant and amusing. I never saw a more joyous crew, nor a set of human beings who forfeited less of cheerfulness than themselves, for having renounced the pleasures of the world! We drove back to Rome delighted with our expedition, and the next morning reassumed the usual occupation of visiting the antiquities. . . .

The highlight of the stay in Rome was the celebration of Holy Week; the performance of the Miserere in the Pope's Chapel in the Vatican, the glimmering light from the altar flickering on the Last Judgement *of Michael Angelo, so that to Katherine watching, the figures seemed, miraculously, to move; the washing of the feet of twelve ancient pilgrims, and after, the Pope himself serving the twelve at dinner. Holy Week ended with the grand and final ceremony of the Papal benediction on Easter Sunday.*

But I omitted a private transaction, which was our presentation to the Pope. At four o'clock on Good Friday Lady Mount Cashell and I accompanied the Princess Borghese to the gardens of the Vatican where at the end of a long avenue, we beheld Pius VII encircled by his righteous conclave.

He was dress'd in a scarlet large flowing mantle trimmed with gold, scarlet beaver hat bound with gold, scarlet shoes with gold crosses embroider'd on each, and a friar's dress underneath his mantle.

The Princess, as we approach'd his holiness stepp'd forward and throwing herself on her knees, kiss'd his toe. Lady Mount Cashell and I advanced and were half bent to perform the like operation, when, I am grieved to say, the Pope by a motion of his hand dispensed us from this tribute, which we would most gladly have paid. Sincerely disappointed at the compliment, we walk'd with him towards a pavilion into which he walk'd first, tho' this prerogative he made appear as much the effect of accident as possible. Here we sat an hour, extremely pleasant and utterly free from the slightest form of ceremony.

He is more than sixty years of age apparently, with sincere, simple and gentleman-like manners. He talk'd principally, and in Italian, laugh'd at a hundred trifles, and appear'd unfeignedly

81

amused at the desire Lady Mount Cashell express'd to see the Convent of the Capuchins and their cemetery, which is composed of human bones, so arranged as to form separate grottoes. He promised permission should be granted, as well for our seeing that, as the interior of a nunnery and desired the Princess Borghese shou'd send the next day to the Vatican to have the grant signified in due form to the Capuchins.

After conversing good humour'dly for an hour, he got up, the Princess falling on her knees and again kissing his toe and we again attempting the same ceremony, which he would not permit.

On going out of the pavilion into a sort of garden full of hyacinths, pollyanthus, narcissus, orange trees etc., the Pope very gallantly pull'd a hyacinth and gave it to Lady Mount Cashell, and desired one of the cardinals to follow his example, which he did by gathering me a bouquet and presenting it likewise in a very gallant manner.

A dozen servants who were in attendance fell down to their knees the moment his Holiness appear'd and remain'd in that posture till he turn'd into another walk. He and all the cardinals escorted us down the avenue to the carriage and after civilities, and devotional ones on the part of the Princess were at an end, we drove home. I forgot to mention our bless'd beads, made of agate and jasper enchased in gold which he gave us. So ended our visit to his Holiness.

The permission for seeing the Convent of the Capuchins was duly deliver'd, and we drove off there in great triumph, as the Capuchins had many of them assured us, it was impossible for our curiosity to be gratified relative to the cemetery.

A number of them in their cinder-colour'd dress, bare feet, scald heads and grizzly beards, came out to meet us in full grin, and ushered us into their convent.

They threw open all the doors of their cells, which contained each a little bed, crucifix, holy water and bell, and then usher'd us into the refectory, chapels etc.

Amongst various curiosities, they shew'd us a cross made by

the devil and some of Saint Luke's paintings. They then walk'd before us with their prodigious bunch of keys in their hands and descended into the cemetery.

We found ourselves in an endless length of gallery composed entirely of human bones and, to the right, opening into little grottoes form'd of knuckles, ribs, skulls, bones and every vestige of the miserable human frame so curiously and fancifully arranged, as really to produce an uncommonly pretty effect. The chief ornament goggling from the top, being generally a grinning skull and crossbones.

In each compartment, erect against the wall, stood six skeletons in the Capuchin habit with their skins dried tight upon their bones, and their long beards flowing grizzly to their girdles. In their long bony hands they held their beads and at their sides hung the usual insignia of their holy office.

The live monks who conducted us about told us all their names, pointed out who and who were their friends, shew'd us the vacant niches they expected they shou'd fill, and altogether appear'd as little appall'd at the idea of becoming like those horrid grim skeletons, as if the transformation was not to be acquired through the ordeal of death. . . .

We were last of all conducted into the cell of the Superior, who received us with a grace, ease, and dignity so peculiar, that we cou'd think of nothing else. I never saw so striking a being in all my life, and as he stood in his little cell, without a second chair to offer us or one single comfort or luxury of existence, his air inspired a greater reverence and admiration than all the thrones and potentates in Christendom. . . .

The eternal round of variety we are in, saves us in some degree from the effects of the scirocco wind, but still I find it depressing beyond measure. It produces so universal a languor and lassitude, and makes one's very life a burthen.

I was sitting in this debilitated state the other day in my room before breakfast when the door open'd and a priest in full canonical robes appear'd, with a vessel of holy water in one hand, and a long switch in the other, which he dipp'd occasionally into the holy water and sprinkled all about the room, muttering prayers between his teeth and proceeding with his purification without taking the least notice of me no more than if I only form'd part of the furniture.

I almost thought it was the apparition of a wizard and started up to apprize him of my being there. But he only answer'd to this motion, by a shower of holy water in my face and passed on into the adjoining chamber where he continued his works of grace, while I ran off to enquire the cause of his appearance in so questionable a form, and found out it was a religious function to lay evil spirits, of which number he must have imagined me one of no small magnitude if I judged from the splash of holy water I received in such abundance. . . .

On 16 April the Mount Cashell party at last left Rome. A friend, Mr Clifford, kept them company for the first three days as far as Foligno. From Foligno the Mount Cashells went on to Perugia and, via Arezzo, to Florence.

Florence, 10th July, 1803. à l'Aigle Noir.
I have now to account for a sojournment here of ten weeks. . . . The little child* having had the measles, and Lady Mount Cashell's consequent long illness have been the cause of our not returning into France, or at least to Geneva, where the rest of the family have been.

This delay has totally prevented our evading the consequences of the war, which has broke out between England and France, the news of which reach'd us the 1st of June, with the aggravation of an embargo being laid on British travellers, to the utter prohibition of the gentlemen's returning to their own countries. . . .

The prohibition was to prove disastrous for some. Maria Edgeworth's brother, Lovell, on his way from Geneva to Paris, had been warned of the

---

* Lady Mount Cashell's new baby.

possible state of affairs by his father. But not receiving the letter, he was made a prisoner and remained among the détenus *for eleven years. Fanny Burney was also affected, though to a lesser extent. Having joined her husband in France, she was not to see England again for ten years. Meanwhile the itineraries of English travellers on the Continent were drastically revised. Miss Berry, along with her sister, her father and their dog, had to return, like Katherine Wilmot, through Germany.*

As for the Mount Cashells, their children had been left behind at Nîmes with Mr Egan, the boys' tutor, and Mrs Ruaud, the governess of the girls. Fortunately the children were later taken to Geneva for safety, though Mr Egan was imprisoned by the French.

'To Kitty this will not be a matter of much concern'[3] her sister Matty had commented when she heard the news of the French internments of foreigners, and from Katherine's subsequent tranquil occupations, and amused comments in the journal, this seems to have been the case.

During Lady Mount Cashell's illness, I have for the first time this age had time to read and write a little, and for the first time I got through the works of Florian,* which I was tired with telling everybody 'I never had read'.

I went on with shepherds and shepherdesses, Estelles, Merils, Nemorins, Galatees, Chloes, and Myrtles till I felt myself growing into a crook, and I believe if I was to read on for a week longer I should lose my speech, and bleat like a sheep.

I wish I could possess the sense necessary to relish the society of so many flocks and herds. Swift to me is more amusing, who makes man an etcetera to horses, than Florian who makes them one to sheep. At least I would choose to be the *valet de chambre* of a nag rather than a ram. . . .

Everybody dines here at two o'clock, and then goes to bed. At six they get up and dress themselves, and drive off to the Cascina, where they talk to each other from their carriage windows, but seldom or never walk. The place is fragrant with baskets of carnations, mignonette, yellow roses, and orange

---

* Jean Pierre Claris de Florian (1755–94), French poet and writer of romances.

blossoms in bouquets which everybody buys, and on returning home, 'tis the custom to stop and eat ice, and then go off to the theatre, or *conversaziones*, or any engagement one has at home.

We very often walk out on the bridges and quays by moonlight, which is the fashion and one of the greatest of refreshments possible, after the relaxation of a hot day, the streets are full of musicians, who sing in parts as they walk about, and serenade their friends.

I never saw anything like the beauty of the fire flys, which I can compare to nothing less brilliant than stars, and they really look fully as beautiful, when they fly in swarms about the garden by night. Night in this country surpasses anything, for splendour, I ever witness'd anywhere. For the last six or seven weeks I have never taken any exercise except during the hours of ten, eleven and twelve. There is a garden belonging to a Florentine family with whom I am very intimate, where I go almost every evening to walk. It is a wilderness of sweets, and as we sit in a white jessamine arbour, looking at the glory of the heavens, the glittering of the fire flys amongst the rose bushes, and inhaling the fragrance of the orange flowers, I declare I often forget that imagination has not supplanted reality and that I am not an inhabitant of the world of poets. . . .

Since the arrival of the courier from Paris to General Clarke,* the French Minister, announcing war, everybody has been in the utmost consternation.

No one knows what is to become of us. Some say we are to be sent home from Leghorn by long sea, in which case we should infallibly die in the Bay of Biscay, or be taken by pirates, if we did not perish from suffocation long before. Others conjecture we are to be sent to Palermo, others that we shall not be permitted to leave Tuscany. Everyone wants to get home, and when one can for a moment forget the awkwardness of our situation, it is excessively laughable to see the long faces everyone makes at his own fantasies.

* Henri Jacques Guillaume, Duc de Feltre (1760–1818), Marshal of France. He was son of Thomas Clarke of Aharney, Queen's Co, Ireland.

I had proposed and frustrated a thousand plans for my return to Ireland. Lord Mount Cashell, I knew, was unable to return during the war, the indefinite length of which precluded all hope. Lady Mount Cashell was peculiarly circumstanced on account of her children being in France, and their tutor a prisoner. There was therefore no chance or probability of her leaving them abroad unprotected by herself. Every soul ran about to know what his neighbour would do before he would determine himself. This state of mind amongst the British in Florence produced a panic and confusion unexampled.

Every house exhibited the strangest tragi-comic scenes imaginable. Ransoms were speculated upon – chains and dungeons glanced at – gentlemen went off in disguise at the peril of their lives – ladies fainted – the Duchess of Cumberland* flew to the Pope's dominions, and three or four families at her heels. Every creature seem'd running helter skelter asking compassion, and receiving the assault of other's woes, as the only responses to his own. How to get home, was the only talisman that struck a common sympathy.

In the midst of these perpetual convulsions, Mrs Clifford appeared from Naples, where we had known her very well, and who kindly allowed me to join her party, as she proposed going through Germany to England. Here then ends my Florentine history!

The miseries of the last few days previous to my parting with Lady Mount Cashell, I will cover with a pall. Two years uninterrupted happiness in her society was obliterated by the anguish of separation. And the morning of my departure, I never more earnestly wished for anything, than that, even by so long a spell of pleasure, I had not incur'd the trials to which I then became a victim.

* Lady Anne Lutrell d. 1803, married in 1771 her second husband, Henry, Duke of Cumberland.

1 – 19 September 1803

The friends never met again, though they corresponded. After Katherine left for England the Mount Cashells managed to reunite their scattered family and take them to Rome. It was at Rome early in the following year that Lady Mount Cashell, bored to death by the dull circle there, met her destiny in the person of George William Tighe.

'. . . at thirty I considered myself perfectly secure from either inspiring or being inspired with the passion of love,'[1] she later wrote. But Mr Tighe proved the exception, and by the time she had given birth to her eighth child that August she knew she was in love.

'A combination of circumstances promoted our intimacy and augmented our admiration of each other,' she tells us, 'neither of us had sufficient resolution to withstand a strong passion and for years we suffered a variety of anxieties and difficulties. Misfortune,' Lady Mount Cashell concluded with pious truth, 'must ever be the lot of those who transgress the laws of social life.'[2]

She continued to live with Lord Mount Cashell, in 1805 even accompanying him to Germany on the way to Ireland. But in Germany her heart failed her, and he returned home alone taking their children with him.

For a time she was, in her own words, 'a vagabond on the face of the earth'.[3] Eventually she settled in Pisa with her lover under the assumed name of 'Mrs Mason', after an admirable character in Original Stories *which had been written long before, by her governess, Mary Wollstonecraft.*

She had two more daughters, became herself an author of improving children's books, a friend of Shelley and his family, and the source of inspiration for his poem, The Sensitive Plant. *She died in Pisa in 1835 aged sixty-two.*

Katherine, meanwhile, had joined her friend, Mrs Clifford, and her invalid son for the long journey back to England. The Cliffords travelled in their own carriage, Katherine in a German barouche specially bought for the occasion, though they interchanged companions between the two carriages three or four times a day.

They made a pleasure of the journey, halted at Vallombrosa, visited Ariosto's tomb at Ferrara and eventually arriving at Venice stayed for a week, Katherine revelling in its beauty and enjoying 'the absence of all bustle and noise, such as addles one in every other town . . .'[4]

From Venice they took eight days to reach Vienna, where they ransacked the sights before passing on to Prague. Here Katherine and her friends ate ices in the public garden, delighted by the Gothic cathedral, the shops, the happy-looking people. By the eighth of August they were in Dresden after an exhausting journey in which the springs of Katherine's coach broke throwing her into the ditch. At Dresden they glimpsed the Elector at church, 'a good looking elderly man in a white uniform', also his wife, 'very vulgar, and on a large scale, as are most of the court'.[5] They also inspected the Treasury Office, 'eight rooms lined with the most expensive and splendid playthings for the Elector'.[6]

By the eighteenth of the month they were in Berlin, having travelled all night, their coaches bursting a passage for themselves through the trackless pine forests. On the way, they stopped at Potsdam to look at Frederick the Great's palace at Sans Souci, and to stare in awe at Voltaire's ink well.

In Berlin their windows in the Hôtel de Russie overlooked the public walk 'where we see all the ladies walking about with a little basket on their arms, instead of a reticule as in France . . .'[7]

Lodging on the same floor was Madame le Baronne d'Eyhenberg, whom they'd met at Dresden and who invited the party to meet Professor Von Schlegel, the famous poet.

Berlin was as thoroughly explored as everywhere else including the Cathedral and the royal palace at Charlottenberg. The Queen was pronounced a perfect beauty, the King reckoned selfish and mean with his money. They stayed there almost a week, and by 29 August had reached the Danish coast. . . .

Denmark, Husum, Duchy of Schleswig, Sepr. 1st, 1803.
We have been four days miserably lodged in this little insignifi-

cant town, which is so full of people going to England, that Mrs Clifford, Mr Clifford, Lord John Campbell and Mr Robertson and I, together with five servants, have had no other accommodations than a little huxter's shop, not much bigger than a nutshell.

On leaving Berlin the 23rd of August, at five in the morning, we were agreeably surprized at seeing Lord John Campbell's* carriage drawn up at the door, and on meeting at the breakfasting inn, it was arranged that we should join parties. We found the country from Berlin during the first day's journey to consist of wild sandy plains resembling the country between Dresden and Bockitz. In the like manner as there, our carriages burst through forests, almost uninterruptedly both day and night.

The second day we were tormented by not getting horses, as the King and Queen were on the road, going to visit the Duke of Mecklenburg Strelitz, the young Queen's father. The hereditary Prince we met travelling on horseback, a fine-looking young man, who was just riding up to one of his father's palaces, Ludwigslust, a country residence. Most of the day we travell'd through sandy plains not hearing the noise of the carriage wheels and found ourselves suddenly in the middle of a field, toss'd at a considerable distance from the carriage.

From Grabow, where we rested part of that night, we set off and got to dinner the third day to Schewerin, which is prettily circumstanced, all surrounded by trees and statues. After dinner we set out again and travell'd through the night, and dined the fourth day at Lubeck, the Principal city of the Hanseatic league, beautifully situated on the Baltic Sea, of which we had a charming view. On quitting Lubeck, we got into Denmark or rather the territories of the Duke of Holstein, and according to custom travell'd all night long.

The fifth morning we got into breakfast at Kiel, so celebrated for its University. . . . The country became a deadflat, and till the middle of the night we did not arrive at Husum.

* Lord John Campbell (1777–1847), later 7th Duke of Argyll.

We just saw the Prince of Denmark, who pass'd through, as we enter'd the town. On driving to the inn, we found it entirely occupied and we were dismiss'd to seek our fortunes elsewhere.

This little huxter's then was the only refuge we had left and even here we could not get beds till the following night, so that we were obliged quietly to content ourselves on the chairs, where we slept very peaceably till morning. We then got up, shook our ears and eat our breakfasts gaily about six o'clock, enquired about ships and found that in four days the *Lark* packet, Captain Thomson, sail'd for England, 'wind and weather permitting'.

Since we quitted Berlin, we have travel'd three hundred English miles, which is a longer way than had we gone to the left a little by Hamburg. However the French troops which over-spread the country prevented us venturing in that direction, and as they were advancing every day, and gaining ground, we flew thus rapidly from them as I have describ'd, both night and day.

This little Husum is not worth speaking of. It is near the river Ow, on the German ocean, totally unprotected by trees, and dismally bleak, bald, cold and wild. Yet our party is so pleasant, so careless of inconvenience, and so uncommonly agreeable, that we have really spent these four days without a conscious-ness of our unpleasant situation – sometimes in playing chess – sometimes in walking on a dyke, conversation, and eternal good spirits. Added to those I have mention'd are the two Mr Fosters, whom we knew at Naples (they are just return'd from a tour to Constantinople and the Greek Isles), Mr du Cain and Mr and Mrs Trimbeg. She a charming little woman from Nuremberg.

Lark Packet, Husum Roads, Sepr. 14th, 1803.
This is the fourteenth day we have been living on board this packet, six miles off Husum at anchor waiting for a fair wind.

In addition to those I have already mention'd, we have had Major Gildberg, a courier from the King of Sweden to the King of England; Mr Berry, and the two Miss Berrys,* their dog and their

* Robert Berry and his two daughters, Mary and Agnes.

femme de chambre; Sir Alexander Seton,* and Doctor and Mrs Marchand; a young Hambourg merchant, and a Hanoverian Officer; which, with servants make up twenty-six independent of the same number of Hanoverian soldiers, who are going over to the Duke of Cambridge. . . .

We have unpack'd everything to get books. The chess board is in unceasing requisition, a solitary pack of cards are worn into flock. In short I will leave you to imagine a life on board ship, spent by a set of freshwater sailors like ourselves, every moment expecting to sail, and giving ourselves a privilege to be discontented, from the uncertainty of our situation. I believe there scarcely ever was a set of people more fortunate in their companions however, than we are. . . .

England.   19th Sepr. 1803.   Southwold in Suffolk.
Here we are at length landed after a voyage of six days and shall proceed to London immediately.

We had been so well season'd to the ship that I scarcely knew when it was beginning to move. At night as we sat on deck the traces of fire which it left in the water, and the luminous bubbles flying off produced a glorious effect as we sail'd along. For two days we imagined ourselves pursued by French cruisers and preparations were made in the most warlike manner, passports, regimentals, letter bags, and everything that could give either public or private information to the enemy, lash'd on deck, ready to throw overboard the moment of their approach. However, at the end of the second day they disappear'd from the horizon.

The day before we landed, there was so dreadful a storm that the main mast split and as the Captain began to be alarm'd for our safety, instead of anchoring at Norwich, we put in here at Southwold, a little sea bathing place on the shore, and now for the first time these two years, the sounds of English again assail

* Sir Alexander Seton, 5th Baronet (1772–1810), an officer in the East India Company's service.

92

my ears. After being shut up in a ship so long, the common comforts of life absolutely appear luxuries to me. Tomorrow we proceed to town.

3

The Visit to the Great Bear

As the *Lark* crept along the Suffolk coast to Southwold harbour
with its exhausted passengers, Martha Wilmot, more than a
thousand miles away in Russia at the Princess Dashkov's, was
writing up her journal:

'The Princess produced from her stores some Moscow silks
and warm stockings. She presented Anna Petrovna and me with
dresses of the former and a couple of pair of the latter . . .'[1]

She had now been in Russia two months, starting her journey
back in June while her sister was still in Paris with the Mount
Cashells. That she had come to Russia in the first place was an
attempt to take her mind off the grief of losing a favourite
brother.

'I wished to be driven into the necessity of exertion,' she
explained to a friend, 'by being thrown into new scenes in a
foreign country; and the animated letters of my sister, who was
then in France, revived a desire for travelling . . .'[2]

It was her father's cousin, Mrs Hamilton, who had made
the seemingly eccentric proposal that Martha should make
the journey to Russia as the guest of her own dear friend, the
Princess Dashkov – 'let her spend a year or two with the Princess
in Russia,' she had advised. It would make her friend, the
Princess, the happiest of women, and Matty would be received
by her 'as a mother and considered as her child. . . .'[3]

To this proposal the Wilmot parents gave anxious agreement,
and by late July 1803 Matty was in St Petersburg. By now,
however, doubt if not dread had replaced pleasurable anticipation at meeting her hostess.

'I was told,' wrote Matty, 'that she lived in a castle situated in a dreary solitude, far removed from the society of any civilized beings, where she was all-powerful, and so devoid of principle that she would invariably open and read the letters which came to me. . . .'[4]

Her hostess was indeed formidable. Forty-one years before, at the age of nineteen, she had played a decisive part in the coup d'état which had removed the Czar Peter from the Imperial throne in favour of Catherine his Empress.

On the day itself, the young Catherine and the even younger Princess Dashkov, in uniforms of officers in the Preobrazhenski Regiment, had ridden at the head of a twelve-thousand-strong army. At Krasny Kabak, six miles from St Petersburg, they halted, exhausted, and for a few hours the Princess and her future Empress shared the only bed in a filthy inn. Not to sleep however. As the Princess listened, the new Empress read out the manifestos she intended to publish when they returned to St Petersburg.

Safely ensconced in her new role the Empress, depressingly, withdrew her favour over the next seven years. The Princess, it seems, may have claimed too great a part in her triumph; at all events her position was becoming untenable and she went abroad. In Europe she was greeted ecstatically as intellectual and liberator, especially by the cognoscenti, who included Diderot and Voltaire. In England, where for two months her son went to Westminster School, Horace Walpole made a special point of meeting her: '. . . well worth seeing,' he wrote, 'not for her person, though, for an absolute Tartar, she is not ugly: her smile is pleasing, but her eyes have a very Catiline fierceness. Her behaviour is extraordinarily frank and easy. She talks on all subjects, and not ill, nor with striking pedantry, and is quick and very animated. She puts herself above all attention to dress, and everything feminine, and yet sings tenderly, and agreeably, with a pretty voice.'[5]

By the time the Princess returned to Russia the mood of the Empress had softened. For the next six years she wrote articles in various learned periodicals, published translations from the philosopher Hume, passionately collected books, travelled once more to her beloved Europe, placing her son for his education at Edinburgh University.

At the end of this period, by now internationally famous, she returned to Russia once more. The Empress, all complaisance, invited the Princess to become the first Director of the Russian Acadamy of Science; approved of the Princess's suggestion that there should be also a Russian Academy devoted to literature and philosophy. The star of the Princess was once more in the ascendant.

The service of despots, however, is hazardous. It was not long before the Empress was infuriated by the Princess's Academy Press publishing a play in which she thought she could detect unpleasing Jacobinical leanings. The Princess was obliged to retire once more to her country estates. Two years later, on the death of the Empress, the new Czar Paul, who considered the Princess responsible for the overthrow and death of his father, stripped her of her official position and had her exiled to a distant spot in the marshes of Novgorod.

In time she returned to her beloved estate at Troitskoe, and on the death of Paul and the accession of the Czar Alexander, she was once more offered her old appointments. But by now the Princess had lost her faith in Princes, and though by her reinstatement she was once more a person of power and consequence, she preferred retirement on her country estate where she built walls, planted trees, supervised the ailments of her serfs, and improved her agriculture, though without the heart she had once had for such pursuits.

It was at this moment in her life that the Princess met Martha Wilmot.

Martha herself with pronounced Gothic undertones was to recall this meeting.

'It was not till the evening . . . that we arrived, and I beheld with terror the solitary castle, the scene of my threatened imprisonment. At last the sorceress appeared! She wore a long

96

cloth coat, with a large silver star on the left side; her head-dress was a man's nightcap, and round her neck was a coloured silk handkerchief, which *friendship* had consecrated to the same use for more than twenty years. It was the gift of Mrs Hamilton, to secure her from cold one evening, and she would never, in her evening walks, wear any other. . . .'[6]

The eyes of the elderly Princess and the young Irishwoman met. '. . . before she had uttered a word, except "Welcome," ' wrote Matty, 'I felt I loved her more than any one I had seen since I quitted my own family. . . .'[7]

It was a feeling passionately reciprocated.

Matty, like her sister Katherine, kept a journal. It was not long before bulletins to her mother, her father, her younger sisters, were winging their way home to Glanmire.

There were pensées on the Russian character – 'very clever, quick as thought at catching an idea, faithful copiers of any new invention . . . excellent thieves'.[8] There was her account of how in Moscow she had met the notorious Count Alexis Orloff,* assassin of the Czar Peter. He wore the Empress's picture set in diamonds 'of enormous size, and instead of a glass, 'tis a single diamond which covers the portrait'.[9] She went on to report him a monster in appearance, his strength almost beyond belief. In lighter vein she told them how she had gone 'ice hilling', racing down ice chutes boxed in with fir branches – 'I should think the sensation must resemble the flight of a bird . . . I went seven times.'[10]

In quieter mood she evoked days back at Troitskoe with the Princess, reading, discussing politics, literature, the past, 'those calm pleasures,' as the Princess herself later wrote, 'which a long want of something to unite my affections and call forth the powers of my mind had now rendered doubly dear to me'.[11]

Two years slipped by. Napoleon abandoned the invasion of England, Pitt assembled the third coalition against him,

---

* Count Alexis Orloff-Chesmensky (1735–1807). During the revolution of 1762 he took the deposed Czar Peter III to the Castle of Ropscha and murdered him.

97

Napoleon had himself crowned King of Italy, Austria joined the Anglo-Russian Alliance. Back at Glanmire the Wilmot family grew restless, and it was at last proposed that Katherine, no doubt fired in her turn by her sister's accounts of Russia, should travel out and bring Matty home. It was not long before the plan was endorsed by a warm invitation from the Princess.

On Saturday 8 June 1805, Matty noted '5 letters from home containing the happy intelligence that my sister *will* indeed come. . . .'[12]

On 13 July she wrote to her mother that she and the Princess were waiting to hear the probable time of Kitty's arrival in Russia, and that the Princess had sent off a huge trunk to Moscow containing 'various silks, satins, Russ napkins and etc. to greet her'.[13]

On 12 August they heard Katherine had landed at Cronstadt. Curiously enough, her arrival in Russia more or less corresponds in time with the opening of Tolstoy's great novel, *War and Peace*. In the novel, however, it is July 1805, and at Anna Scherer's soirée the guests are discussing Napoleon's outrageous execution of the Duc d'Enghien for conspiracy.

As in *War and Peace* (a phrase Katherine reports as being on all lips), the background to Katherine's Russian visit was the war of the third coalition. Three months later the coalition was broken apart by the defeat of the Austrian and Russian armies at Austerlitz, and two years after that the Russian armies were crushed at Friedland.

It was thus the society of the Bezukhovs, the Rostovs, and Bolkonskis, as described by Tolstoy, that Katherine was to meet and herself describe (not flatteringly) in her journal and her letters home. It is this that gives her Russian journals particular interest, for she was a highly intelligent and perceptive observer.

Other travellers had of course preceded her to Russia, though they were few and far between compared to those who had described the well-known countries of western Europe.

For one thing Russia appeared boundless.

'This great Northern Monarchy,' the Rev. William Mavor had written in his *Universal History* of 1802, 'exceeds the limits of the largest and most celebrated empires of antiquity, in the zenith of their power and glory . . .'[14] He added somewhat pedantically, that in breadth the Empire was 2,400 English miles, in length 9,200.

Rather earlier, in 1783, William Richardson had given some interesting insights into the character of the Russian people. 'Desultory and inconsistent,'[15] he had remarked of them, in their happy moments displaying themselves in 'infantine levity', their lows frequently terminating in suicide. Though able to express the most ardent affection in the most ardent language (for which their own was eminently suited), they, alas, had more sensibility than firmness, were hopelessly unsubdued by reason.

The Russian peasant, he allowed, was handsome in a dark sort of way, the women gay, though sadly ill-proportioned, living on black bread, garlic and fish. The men, he noted, had the universal habit of greeting one another with extravagantly low bows, and he recalled two such, who saluting one another in a hard frost, had got their beards entangled and subsequently fast-frozen together.

The Russ amusements Mr Richardson had found to be of an indolent kind, viz. singing, drinking, swinging on see-saws and sliding down ice-hills in the winter. Of the machinations of the secret police by which the Czar kept order, he was of course, as an Englishman, highly critical, as he was of the enslaved state of the peasants. The wealth of great Russian magnates was not counted in land, he reported, but in slaves. 'The Prince Sherebatoff has 127,000,'[16] he wrote. He also noted the surprising fact that 'a nobleman is here nothing; his situation in the army alone marks the value of his existence'.

Katherine Wilmot had read Mr Richardson either before or after arriving in Russia, since his *Anecdotes of the Russian Empire* is included on her reading list along with several others.

William Coxe, fellow of King's, was also on her list. He gave a somewhat graver account of what he saw on his Russian visit, an account well illustrated with facts and figures and sober comment, endorsing much of what Richardson had already remarked. But although, like most travellers, he was to judge Russia by progressive eighteenth-century standards, he did particularly notice the popular music of the people. For the most part, though, he praised Russian hospitality; admired the enormous city of Moscow with its glittering spires and domes, 'certainly the largest town in Europe'; approved of the English gardens that he saw and the copy of Vauxhall put up by the enterprising Mr Mattock. He also noted, surprisingly, that polite Russians appeared not to be 'wedded to the bottle', like their English counterparts, since they retired from the dinner table along with the ladies.

With his calculations and tables of exported Russian goods, he was able to gauge the great potential of the country, though from the point of view of progress considered it still in the state Europe had been in the eleventh and twelfth centuries. None the less he noted that enlightened Russians were at last beginning to question both the morality and enervating effects of slavery.

Not so Lady Craven who, accompanied by a large harp, was travelling to Constantinople by way of the Crimea. In her published travels (also read by Katherine), she argued that 'a people who are in a manner the property of their lord, suffer many of the afflictions that attend slavery, but the very circumstance of their persons being their property insures them the indulgence of their master for the preservation of their lives . . .', adding that it made her laugh to ponder 'the ridiculous ideas of liberty and property that our English common people have . . .'[17]

Her views, as we shall see, were not shared by Katherine.

Like all these previous travellers Katherine initially followed the accepted itinerary – Cronstadt, St Petersburg, Moscow, with all their relevant curiosities and delights. Unlike them, however, and by virtue of being the guest of Princess Dashkov, more and stranger doors were opened to her. Though it was the response from within herself, as a consequence of her Irishness perhaps, which ensured that by way of observing the personalities, the customs, the religions and the myths of that great country, she could approach as no others had done, its beating heart and secret soul.

4

Russian Journal

4 – 31 August 1805

4th of August 1805 [To her sister Alicia]
On board the *Good Intent* lying before the fortifications of Cronstadt in the Mole.

This day three weeks we left London and at 6 o'clock this morning we anchor'd in Russia! Now my dear A. I may as well fold up my letter for as I am a state prisoner on board ship and have only taken a few observations through the telescope on deck, I have only to communicate that the stonework of the forts and batteries here is remarkably handsome and impregnable, that the men of war are excessively ornamental and numerous, and that the Mole is fill'd with merchantmen, which I fear very much will retard considerably our operations.

The water is quite alive with little boats returning from Peterhoff where last night, in consequence of the Empress Dowager's birthday, fêtes, masquerades etc. etc. etc. were held for her honor and glory. A country palace surrounded with woods call'd Oranienbaum borders the opposite shore.

This is all I see of Russia, excepting (of its inhabitants) two Custom House officers who came the moment we anchor'd and seal'd up our trunks, and now a soldier who stays on deck to watch that nothing contraband is convey'd away from the ship till we get under way for Petersburg. The Captain, good man, is gone on shore to see what can be done, but as this is Sunday I fear nothing very effective from the agent can be expected.

Well to be sure, I little thought that the first thing I should have to complain of in Russia was *heat* but it is insufferable! The boats have got awnings over them, and I observe that this soldier on deck has nothing but trowsers and a linen great coat to guard him from the inclemency of the weather. . . . Since we left Elsineur we have scarcely felt the motion of the ship, and the evening we quitted it, sailing up the sound like lightning, Copenhagen, which is washed by the waves, flitted by us like a scene in a magic lantern, the floating batteries still lying before it as in 1801 when Lord Nelson gain'd the battle!

This was the last object we saw, tho' land often appear'd at either side of the vessel, and almost through the Cattegat the water was nearly fresh. Buoys, light-houses, rocks, seals tumbling about the ship, and sometimes a nook of an island seen through the telescope were the only interruptions to the Gulph of Finland. Nine long days have we been navigating that sometimes dangerous pass.

I don't well know how to account for the time. The day on board ship is cut up by dining at two o'clock. Eleanor* sat on deck and made me up a gown, in general she was sick when it was possible. I amused myself sometimes with reading *Mme de la Vallière*, sometimes books on navigation belonging to the Captain, sometimes *Les Mères rivales*, sometimes in reforming a reprobate cabin boy who is on the high road to the gallows, sometimes with the horses in the hold, then hearing of battles from the sailors. So, reading, working, and sleeping like a top. Our woes ended this morning at six o'clock by anchoring at Cronstadt.

Sunday evening.
The Captain interrupted me by a letter from Matty (written this day two months from Troitskoe†) which he received from Mr Booker, the English agent at Cronstadt. The Princess seal'd it with a seal. She had had engrav'd on purpose a large 'Welcome'

* Eleanor Cavanagh, Katherine's maid.
† Princess Dashkov's country estate.

and says in the inside, 'My sentiments you can discover in that word upon the Seal'.

Mr Booker wrote me a most kind note and sent it by his cousin who came on board to deliver it. It was to invite me to dinner and to offer his services. I wrote to him in return refusing the *Mutton* part of his friendship but enclosing letters for him to forward to Moscow.

The Princess has had a letter written to General Koroffko, who resides at Cronstadt to shew me every species of attention and another to Admiral Hannicoff, who resides there, but I believe I shall not apply to either. My whim is to stick like a rat to the ship till it arrives in Petersburg, for excepting the docks Cronstadt would not indemnify* me for any trouble and those I can see at my leisure. At least this is my present determination.

Matty tells me that the Princess has written a flattering letter of introduction to her niece Madame de Poliansky for me, and I am to be at her house while I am at Petersburg, also to Madame de Tchitchagoff, wife to the first Admiral and Minister of the Marine. I am likewise to be introduced to Mademoiselle de Kotchetoff, a niece of the Princess, maid of honor to the Empress. I will now put this by as I suppose I must enclose the statue of Peter the Great, or you would not release my letter from the Post Office; so I'll go walk on deck and view the fortifications.

Wednesday [7th August, 1805] St. Petersburg, at Mr. Raikes's.
Late last night I arriv'd in this magnificent looking town. Monday morning Mr Booker sent his carriage to the Mole, and Mr Whitlock† accompanied Ellen and me to his house in Cronstadt where he received us most hospitably and sent us in his carriage to undergo the usual examinations at the Admirality. We then return'd to dine at his house where he

* Compensate.
† Mr Whitlock was a merchant at Cronstadt who had been on the voyage from England.

insisted on our taking up our quarters while we remain'd at Cronstadt. In the evening we walk'd to see the beautiful docks and return'd to sup in the garden where we remain'd till midnight. I never felt weather in Italy more intolerably hot than this, and the musquetoes are agonizing!

Yesterday morning Mr Booker put us into a barge, and giving us a trusty conductor sent us across to Oranienbaum, eight versts,* where a carriage and another trusty conductor from Mr Raikes† met us with a letter of invitation from Mrs R. to beg I shou'd make her house my home at Petersburg. . . .

The moon rose as yellow as gold over the black forests and conducted us on to Petersburg where we arriv'd at near eleven o'clock. I was in a perfect extacy with all I had seen! All the family of the Raikes's were assembled in the balcony and flew downstairs to meet us. We were then conducted up to the balcony where all sorts of civility pass'd and where I saw the *reach* of this street (if so it may be call'd), the Neva running between this and the opposite houses which is the handsomest river I ever saw in any town.

I forgot to tell you I got a second letter from Matty written only a fortnight ago. It is full of messages of the most affectionate nature from the Princess who has put matters in train for me to be hoop'd out and presented at Court. I am going to write a note to Madame Poliansky, who resides near here, to inform her of my arrival. The Princess wishes me to reside at her house while I am in town, and Madame P. has written the handsomest invitations. I am to delay therefore for a fortnight at Petersburg and then proceed to Moscow. Trusty servants and travelling carriages are to be provided for me. In short, my way indeed is strewed with flowers, for what with the affection of the Princess and her influence everything is *smack smooth* and I have only to repel politeness.

I have written an expostulatory letter to the Princess on the

---

* A verst = two-thirds of a mile.
† Mr Raikes was a merchant in St Petersburg.

subject of her coming to Moscow* in this melting weather which Matty says is a sacrifice to welcome and hospitality, partiality and good fellowship far beyond anything I can have conception of. Already a fox fur pelisse of the rarest kind is provided for my bones and sundry peices of satin together with a sarsenett dress for my squire!† I expect this year to be a fairy tale. Here my friend and conductor old Whitlock leaves me. My friends have work'd him through all his difficulties and now he goes to Archangel.

The bugs and musquetoes punish us severely. I have slept on chairs without any covering *save my chemise* these two nights. While I write my eye is attracted by the sight of academies, palaces etc. etc. etc. etc! Oh, but the men servants do so amuse me! They every one have the oddest appearance. They look as if a Turk had been their father and a Quaker their mother! I cannot describe their appearance any other way. The sound of the language here is soft and agreeable.

And so adieu.

It was now the 'squire's' turn to relay her own impressions‡ of St Petersburg, and the trials and wonders of being a guest in the house of Madame Poliansky, the Princess's niece.

Petersburg, August 20th 1805
Miss Henrietta!§

While I was in the ship one night (turning round in my bed) I laugh'd to myself to think the time down in the village that you bid me send my love to you all the way from Russia, and I'll engage I thought of it often enough both by sea and land! 'Tis likely enough you wou'd have got it by the letters Miss Wilmot

---

* From her estate, sixty miles away, to welcome Katherine.

† Eleanor.

‡ The style is reminiscent of the servant's letters home in Smollett's novel, *Humphrey Clinker*.

§ Henrietta, younger daughter of the Rev. John Chetwood of Glanmire, County Cork, and sister-in-law of Martha and Katherine Wilmot.

writes. But I'd be asham'd to put in my own words,* and since you ask'd me to tell you how I lik'd Russia (when once I was out of Ireland) 'tis the plainest way to slip in this bit of a letter that will be unseal'd by yourself in Glanmire. . . .

I did not think so bad of the voyage at all, because I was not half so sick as in the ship coming from Ireland! We stop'd in Denmark at Elsineur, and all the sea was cover'd over with ships like a wood!† 'Twas very pleasant! As to that we had but two stormy days of all the passage. Signs by, I sat out and made a gown while we were going along.

Everything was very nice in the ship; the captain was a very good sort of captain, and plenty of hens to lay fresh eggs, and a room with two beds to ourselves. We could get everything from James (the steward) through the little window out. Indeed the captain and above all the old gentleman and the servant who did everything like the father of a family ('Twas he who took care of us from London) were good natured. I think nothing of being at sea, tho' they say we sail'd 1500 miles of ground.

I never was so surpris'd as to see Mr Booker's carriage at Chronstadt (where we anchor'd in Russia) drive down to the shore for us to take us up to his house! 'Twas because the coachman had a *quair* long sash and a black beard and a coat plaited about the man's waist, may I never stir! like a petticoat. The Lord be praised there were English maid servants there, and indeed they were very civil, and a fine set of children belonging to the lady of the house!

Ogh! my God! to see the country women! Why wou'dn't they content themselves to dress like Christians? Miss Henrietta, 'twou'd sour one to look at the craitures with their blue and yellow and green cloth petticoats bound with gold, and bouncing bobs of *air-rings*‡ in their *airs* and shift sleeves like men's shirt sleeves! I'll engage they wou'dn't forget their *baid* necklaces!

---

* Into Miss Wilmot's letter!
† She means their clustered masts.
‡ Earrings.

'Twou'd make one ashamed to think how they'd ape the quality! Better for them wash their faces and not have so many flaighs* hopping about them. That I mighten'd but it wou'd!

'Twas two days after we went that we quit Mr Booker and sail'd eight miles across to a fine palace. God knows I wou'dn't know the name, off it wou'dn't be Orangenbaum! There another coach and two servants with ugly beards (one of them as red as a rose) came to take us thirty miles on to Petersburg! Why, wou'd you believe it ma'am, they put four long tail'd horses all in a row and then two again at the end of long rope traces (and they seldom cuts the manes of them at all, for down they hang in bushels of plaits, or else without them)! And Ogh! my God! to hear the smack and the cry that the postillions give, and how they drive like smoke up the hills! That I mighten'd! but I made full sure to myself that we were fairly out of Ireland then!

I never see anywhere in Glanmire such a shew of palaces and big woods as them all by the country at either side while we drove along. *Images*, out upon the roofs with wings growing out of them as natural as a bird. If it was not that I seen one on one of the gentlemen's hielst† ('twas he that had a big *corkscrew* in his hand, and by that I knew it might be the country where all the wine comes from), I was tired of reckoning and looking at them, and the summer houses, and the elegant green lawns, and the loads of roses and geraniums, all out of doors! 'Twas well we came in the evening for the days are killing hot, and the sun here I believe is a bigger and more scalding one than in Ireland!

I'll never forget how beautiful Petersburg look'd the first day. Cork is a *flay* to it, and the river as large as the Lee five times over. I don't believe they call it by that name tho'. We slept that night at Mr Raikes's in a great church of a house, very civil people, and all as one as Mr Read or Mr Anderson down at Fermoy!

They gave me plenty of *convaniencies* to wash out the things we dirted in the ship, and indeed the soap too was good enough. I'll

---

* Fleas.
† Eleanor is describing a statue of Mercury; 'hiels' are heels.

engage I got *tai* and fine *craim* (and plenty of it) for my breakfast, and Miss Raikes's maid give me a nice border of a lace cap and Miss Wilmot's white wrapper dress'd me up smart enough to go with the servants of the house down to see the palace.

I thought the screech wou'd have choak'd me when turning round my head what wou'd I see leaping over a *rail* rock but a giant of a man on the back of a *dragin* of a horse.

'Stop him!' says I, (for I declare to God, Miss Henrietta, but I thought the life wou'd have left me to see a live Christian making such a fool of himself) when what did I hear but that he was a *marble Emperor*! Some old snake of a man that they call Peter, or Peter the Great, or something like that!

The next day Madam Poliansky (a fine black eyed pleasant young lady niece to the Princess Daschkaw) sent off her carriage for us. It was at night that we arriv'd here at her house, and I had a dread over me to walk through so many ball rooms as the Blackamoor with a yellow jacket and a turban and a couple of candles in his hands made us go through. Many a gown might Nurse Connell get out of the crimson damask that the walls are paper'd with!

Ogh, but the flies bit us all night long!! I was wishing for Mary Hurley (and Mistress Hurley too for the matter of that) to see the sight I seen when I woke in the morning!

'Carry me out,' says I. 'Who are you with your gold tossals and star upon your stomach and crown upon your head?'

She had her eyes right fix'd upon mine, and close enough. She watch'd me wherever I turn'd. They say she too is an Emperor of Russia, and there she hangs in a gold frame as if she was alive.

'Ma'am,' says I to Miss Wilmot, 'what time do they breakfast in this *quair* place?'

The word was hardly out of my mouth when *thump*! a rap comes to the door and in walk'd a grenadier of a man with a silver tray and coffee pot and two cups and saucers and a great *haip* of rusks not on a plate at all, and after him streal'd in at his heels a girl with a bit of a note to Miss Wilmot from her mistress to ask her whether she wou'd like a melon for her breakfast! Oh!

109

then, why wou'dn't the poor thing clap a handkerchief about her yellow neck and not make a lady of herself with her lockets and trash!

Says I to her, 'If we were in Cork now they'd give us a fresh egg!' With that she was so struck that she went out of the room shaking her head, *but the Sarah* an egg came at all*! Why Ma'am here they wou'd as soon think of flying as eating their breakfasts together.

The next day (above at Mr Raikes's where I went to bring a bedgown that I left behind) the young English woman and her brother left me in the passage while they went for their hats, when up comes a Russian with a black beard like a horse's tail and putting his back against the wall he *stud* and said nothing at all. The inside of me sour'd at the sight of him and there he *stud* as grand as twopence.

'Tis a shame Sir,' says I, 'that you don't shave off that horsetail that's hanging from your chin and not leave it there to frighten the people.' With that I look'd at him as bitter as soot.

On he put his clean pair of white linen gloves (not minding a word I said) and then began to tighten his culgee of a fring'd sash about his waist. Out we went, and who shou'd I see but the beard following the young woman and her brother and me.

'I'd be ashamed to walk the streets of Cork with the likes of you,' says I, and look'd as black as a sweep. With that they all laugh'd, and I came home and told it all to my mistress.

'Tis a pleasure to see the plenty of rooms there is to the bed chambers! The three we have to ours are all full of glass and gold, and white marble tables, and a harp, and a harpsichord, and stoves up to the ceiling with gold angels upon them, and a clock that plays eight tunes of itself, and all the floors are made of square peices of *mahogomy* or something like it. . . .

Every day at dinner the life almost leaves me with laughing when I look up at the blackamoor who brings me up my dinner.

'Give me a bit of bread,' says I.

* Sirrah!

110

'*Glep*,' says he (for the craiture don't know to call it by its right name).

'Well then give me *Glep* if that's your fun,' says I again and tho' he talks that way it is as surely *bread* as any in Ireland.

We have music enough all over this house. Eight men servants sit down with their flutes and fiddles. They call them slaves tho', but never a bit of a chain do I see hanging about them any way.

You'd like to see the beautiful new gown I've got, and my mistress's sister is to make me the present of a silk one just out of the shop and a silver crucifix that was made a present to me and a green silk bonnet that I bought myself. I am very happy and likes my place very much. And Miss Henrietta, if you'll go down to the village you may tell my father and mother that I often thinks of their advice and follows it, and remember me to Mrs Mann. Why I sometimes think 'tis only to put on my hat and cloak and down I might run to the village, when I look out of the window and see's Russia again before my eyes.

I went to three of their churches here and they are the same as our chapels as to all I see (but there is one of ours here all the same) and Miss Wilmot knows a Roman who she has spoken to to send a *clargy* here for me to confess to. 'Tis for you to tell my people below in the village that I mention it. I never goes out without *laive*, and every morning I walk with Miss Wilmot half a mile to the cold bath at seven o'clock before breakfast. Last Sunday I was out all day with a very civil English family, and Miss Henrietta, will you *plaise* to tell them down below that I never makes free with any body, nor won't.

One might bid one of them 'Come here!' loud enough, but like fools they stand grinning unless one says 'Paddy Suddy!' and then they bounce up and run as fast as anything, 'tis true for me!

Why now Miss Henrietta, wou'dn't it be enough to turn one's heart into a curd fairly to hear them say *Da* instead of *Yes* and *Niet* instead of *No*. But their *aiting** is good enough, and a *dail* of

* Eating.

111

it, and fruits of all kinds. They brought me in a plate of ice and flump'd a big lump of it in my tumbler glass of wine and water. I thought my heart wou'd be broke in telling them I wasn't used to it, but in they flounc'd another. I'll engage they thought they were making it as strong as whisky.

Give my love Ma'am to Mr Hayes the butler, and the ladies, and above all things to Master Edward, and to Mrs Kanailly of the public house. I'd be sorry to go back *so soon as now*, for to be sure this is a wonderful grand place and I'm always very merry tho' I'm often thinking of everybody in Ireland when I wou'd be sitting at my work. . . .

Give my love to Nancy Thornton and Julia and Anne, and all the sarvants, and indeed Mr Roach was always mighty good to me and I'm following his advice, and to give my respects to Mr and Mrs Wilmot (if they wou'dn't be angry) and the young ladies.

I like to think of you very much, Miss Henrietta, and wou'd be glad you wou'dn't forget me no more than I'd forget yourself. . . .

Eleanor's mistress with a mixture of curiosity and tedium was now presented at the Imperial Court to enable her to move smoothly into Society as the Princess's guest.

But as she was writing up her experiences, on 26 August, 100,000 Russian troops were moving to rendezvous with the Austrian army against the French on the borders of Bohemia.

It was the beginning of the campaign that by December was to result in the defeat of the Russian and Austrian armies at Austerlitz.

St. Petersburg. August 26th [1805], chez Madame Poliansky [to her sister Harriet]
On my arrival the 4th of this month at Cronstadt I received a letter containing a request from Princess D. that when I came here I should be presented at Court. She also wrote to her niece Madame de P. to arrange matters for the ceremony. Unluckily the Court was at Peterhof, and as an opportunity occur'd for me

to go on to Moscow, I declin'd the Imperial honor intended me. The Emperour and Empress came however to Petersburg, and the opportunity of going to Moscow fail'd, from a *wisp* of circumstance too troublesome to disentangle in a letter, so that I was left without any excuse, and therefore my name was given in to the Countess Protassoff, Dame d'Honneur for a presentation. This delay lost me eight days, and till yesterday the Imperial Operation was not perform'd.

Two days before I went in *full puff* with Madame de P. to make an acquaintance with the Countess Protassoff who was to present me. And yesterday at twelve o'clock you may fancy me *toss'd out* in a dress of white crape and roman pearls and white cameo ornaments, my nob *catamomfricated* by a French hair dresser (as I chose myself) with scarlet larkspur to the front. (I suppose it would not be worth a pin if I did not give you this description.)

Well Miss H– *there* I was driven full speed in a coach and six to the Palace of the Tauride (a lovely place as I ever beheld) and conducted by Madame de P.'s servants into an immense marble hall (larger than a church Miss H–) full of statues and columns. You will think it extraordinary that I went *by myself* but it was the etiquette! much as I expostulated with Madame de P. and Madame de Scherbenin (Princess D.'s daughter) and everyone I knew.

From the hall a dozen servants conducted me into a sumptuous looking apartment full of officers in Stars through which I pass'd, and so to another which was empty and which led to the room of presentation. Two lords in waiting rose up, and one of them (in the white uniform of the Horse guards with a crimson order and half a dozen Stars) very politely began to speak French to me. One other Lady had arriv'd before me.

Presently in flourish'd General Kutusow*, uncle to Madame de Poliansky, who is Chief in command of the troops just

---

* Prince Michael Kutusow-Smolensky (1745–1812), Russian soldier and diplomat. Disregard of his advice resulted in the disastrous campaign ending at Austerlitz later in 1805. Later he was largely responsible for Napoleon's retreat from Moscow.

marching against the French, and whom I had known. He is a most respectable old gentleman and I felt quite at ease at having him for a sanctuary. Then in came a lady bowing like a man, 'tis the old Russian mode of salutation, with a diamond cypher on her left breast, and in ten minutes afterwards a pretty little girl looking very modest and like a victim. We all then began to talk to one another, to walk about the room, and to look at the beautiful garden in which the Palace is situated.

After having waited three quarters of an hour, at length an opposite door open'd, and thence came the Empress Elizabeth* follow'd by the *fat* Countess Protassoff at her heels. The Empress is the loveliest creature I almost ever saw and in both face and figure excessively like the print of *Cordelia*, King Lear's daughter. At her entry the ladies rose and the gentlemen retired.

She was dress'd in white embroidery and immense pearls in her beautiful light brown hair. She has the humility, modesty, and sweetness of an angel in her demeanour, and when we were presented and would fain have kiss'd her hand she struggled from the ceremony and in her turn stoop'd down and kiss'd our cheeks. She spoke French to all, excepting one Russian lady to whom she spoke Russ.†

Her voice is very sweet and low, and she speaks as quick as lightening. Appropriate *trifles* were all of course she utter'd. She ask'd me how I lik'd Petersburg and hoped it 'had given me a good impression'. I said it had! (was not that witty?). She said she had heard of my sister at Moscow, and that she understood I intended soon to take a long journey for the gratification of seeing her. I said 'yea'! and that I only delay'd at Petersburg for the honor of being presented to her Imperial Majesty. She then bow'd, and after staying about quarter of an hour, all parties standing in a semi-circle by her, she withdrew with a mob of attendants at her heels. Lovely interesting elegant creature that she is!!

* Wife to the Emperor Alexander.
† Russian.

Sunday 27th August [1805]

I am grievously vex'd for I find I am knock'd down for a further delay. After being presented to the young Empress, I understand it is the indispensable etiquette to go through the same ceremony with the Dowager Empress, for which purpose Madame Poliansky presented me to Princess Prosorofsky last night who said she would report me to her Imperial Majesty and let me know the day. This Princess Prosorofsky is *dame d'honneur* to the Dowager Empress.

On my arrival here Madame de Scherbenin* (Princess Daschkaw's daughter) came off to see me. She is about forty years of age, and an invalid from billious complaints, but looking the picture of health. She is a most perfect woman of the world remarkably cleaver, highly skill'd in languages and mistress of the art of pleasing. I never heard an English woman express herself half so well as she does in English. She has been marvellously civil and kind to me, has made me dine three times at her house, had arranged carriage and servants to attend me to Moscow, which I thought proper to refuse. We have walked *tête-à-tête* in the public walks for hours together, and in fact her politeness is unbounded. Is it not comical? when her mother and she are not on terms, and she was not written to by her about me. . . .†

As to the English here, it is like going into another country to associate with them, for they live entirely amongst themselves. Mr Raikes's house I look upon as a home. I can't describe to you their kindness – they wanted me to stay with them all the time I was at Petersburg, and have got a sweet place in the country that they invite me to perpetually but that I cannot go to.

Mrs Raikes is a young woman married to a *blind cleaver little witch* of a man (Timothy so call'd) of between seventy and eighty. There are little *robins* of looking things, a son and a

---

* Anastasia Scherbenin (1761–1830). She was on bad terms with the Princess, who eventually disinherited her. She died destitute in Moscow.

† She began as a friend, but was to turn into a bitter enemy of Katherine's.

daughter, excessively good natured. But my wonder of a friend in the family is Mrs Raikes's brother, John Cavanagh Esquire.

He is by way of a Lothario, but a merchant to his finger ends, and besides remarkably accomplish'd in sundry languages and general information with a capital headpiece! I inform'd him very expeditiously that I had receiv'd offers of service from *every body*, but to prevent confusion and come to the point, I named *him* my Master of Ceremonies and Bearleader while I stay'd at Petersburg.

Every morning, therefore, he regularly pays me a visit to receive my orders as he says I consider him only as a fagtotum. 'Tis he who has got me the best and cheapest travelling carriage *that ever was seen* and a treasure of a servant who liv'd with him ten years. He puts my letters himself into the office, buys me maps and what I want of every kind in that way, gives me advice as to my steerage in this Russian World, and in short is my guiding star compleatly. He has such a world of affairs on his shoulders that his having accepted my appointment (the Hallidays tell me) I am to consider a singular honor. . . .

Now I have to inform you that since I left London I have never known what it was to catch the slightest cold or ever felt the toothache, so that on the article of health I am very happy. Every morning at seven o'clock I go into the cold bath, and take a vast deal of exercise. I have Petersburg by heart almost – I have a capital map of it, and mounted up to the top of the church in the fortress to look at the town in a glance. The Neva is so magnificent! always full (as it is not subject to the ebb and flow of the tide). I suppose no river in Europe can equal it!

Petersburg is built on a number of little islands, and the country all about perfectly flat, but from the enormous scale on which every thing is built, the new look of the buildings, and the number of public walks and gardens, 'tis difficult to imagine a more beautiful town. And as everybody says, 'tis indeed worthy of being the capital of this prodigious country.

The lower order of people astonish me by their grotesque appearance and the great unmerciful patriarchal beards that the

116

men wear! 'Tis impossible to conceive that they were not born before the Flood, or that their names are not Jacob, Benjeman and Manassus. At the rising and setting of the sun and on other occasions they begin to bow and cross themselves, but so *obstreperously* that the operation does not finish under quarter of an hour. They bow their heads down almost to the ground, and then not only recover their ballance but throw themselves proportionately back again, crossing themselves at arms length. The old women comfortably *kneel* down and kiss the floor, taking the precaution to slip their hands between it and their lips. . . .

Sunday Night 31st August [1805]
After being at Mass I drove in *full puff* to the Palace. Countess Golavine* was there (a charming manner'd woman) and after waiting half an hour in walk'd the Princess Prosorofsky and prepared our minds for the appearance of the Empress Mother. *She* then came in, dress'd in black lace robes and quantities of diamonds in her hair. She is a very fine looking woman, tall and well made, and tho' between forty and fifty having quite the air and appearance of a young woman.

We approach'd towards her as she enter'd (she had one glove off for the operation of kissing), and as we kiss'd her hand she kiss'd our cheeks. She stood and spoke to us (Countess Golavine and me) for five minutes, and then mov'd off to a circle of gentlemen who went through the same ceremony. . . . So now that these Imperial Honors are at an end, I may go off with myself as fast as I chuse. . . .

The travelling carriage which I have got is excellent. It serves for a bed at night (and a most capital one) and has been fitted up for the purpose, having gone a journey before. My two protectors (Frederick and Jerkoff) ride on the dickey which is large enough to hold a third, and the postillions in *full cry* on horseback. I yesterday dined at Madame Sherbenin's and met Dr and Mrs Crighton.† To-day I have spent at Mr Ross's, and the

* Countess Barbara Nicolaevna Golovine (1766–1821), née Princess Galitzen.
† Sir Alexander Crichton (1763–1856), physician in ordinary to the Czar Alexander I.

evening in walking in Count Stroganoff's gardens.

'Tis dreadfully late, and I am very sleepy so my dearest Miss H– adieu! Tomorrow I shall be off for Moscow, thank Heaven. . . . The weather is proving chilly, but I shall have a lovely *moon* for my journey. . . .

9 September – 8 December 1805

The journey took eight strenuous days, and they reached Moscow on 7 September. On the outskirts of the city Katherine halted . . .

I did not chuse to present myself in my travelling dress to the Princess Daschkaw, and besides I had predetermin'd not to arrive at her palace till nightfall (the hour when spirits walk!) so that feeling myself excessively faint from fatigue and hunger, I desired Frederick to get me a little milk, which I presently began to lap at the cottage door, where we stopped, when a smart livery servant with a gold salver, a glass, and sparkling decanter of madeira suddenly appear'd before my eyes!

He pointed to a very handsome looking chateau in the fields, and desired Frederick to explain to me that the Princess Sibersky understood that I was the English lady, on whose account Princess Daschkaw was come to Moscow, and that she felt herself too happy in being the first to welcome me to the gates of Moscow!

The Princess Sibersky stood, waving her hand on the balcony, and the servant was sent backwards and forwards in a dozen courteous messages, as I had to refuse ten thousand civilities she offer'd, amongst the rest accomodation for the night if I felt myself indisposed to proceed further. . . .[1]

Katherine's eventual arrival at the Princess's Moscow palace, where she was to stay three days, was a moment for the sisters almost too painful in intensity of happiness. Certainly sensitive young women, one yet wonders if they were not also, like Jane Austen's Marianne, victims of the smart cult of Sensibility.

Matty recorded this great moment in her journal:

119

'*Tuesday 9th [September 1805]*
'*My precious Kate is arriv'd. Oh my God, excessive joy is a painful thing. K. seeing that there was company here flew up to my room, and one of the servants (Timothy) beckon'd me from the room where I was to tell me the joyful news. I flew and found her greatly agitated.*

"*'Tis two days now since her arrival and I really feel more real bliss in having her than in meeting her, for I was in an agony of joy at first and my darling K. was still worse. We came down to the dearest Princess who came into another room as K. would not face strangers. Never shall I forget the lovely affection of the Princess, dearest kindest of women! Prince D.* likewise came to welcome her, and Anna Petrovna† was highly charmed also and came to tell her so.*

'*We then rush'd into the air and continued walking by bright moonlight till call'd to supper which was serv'd for us in our room. The Princess came as soon as supper was over and she had dismiss'd her guests, and remain'd with us till past one o'clock conversing, after which Kate and I sat up till the blazing sun rose upon our vigil, and shamed me for allowing her, after eight sleepless nights and all the various fatigues of a journey from St Petersburg to Moscow, to sit up in such a manner.*

'*At length sleep closed her eyes, and I began to read some letters from home. However, after going to see that she really was in the very next room to me and that it was no vision or dream, I too fell fast asleep and woke in an extacy the next morning almost doubting my own senses.*'[2]

They crammed in what sight-seeing they could during this first short visit of Katherine's to Moscow; gazed, entranced, at the panorama of the city from Sparrow Mount; saw a bear baiting, which they detested; walked through the Kremlin, and peered into the dungeon which concealed the great Cathedral bell; burst into girlish laughter when Matty had her hand kissed by the Inspector of Police who accompanied them.

For the most part however, Katherine's attention continued to be riveted by the dynamic personality of the Princess.

I will whisk you *nolens volens*,‡ to the handsome Widow

---

* Prince Dashkov, the Princess's son.

† A cousin of the Princess's and her companion.

‡ Whether you like it or not.

Nebalsin's* circular room (so often mention'd in Matty's letters) where Princess Daschkaw in full Star and Garter usher'd Anna Petrovna, Matty and me, after the play. Madame Nebalsin said she was overwhelm'd with mortification at not receiving me at a fête, which she had design'd for my arrival, but which our leaving town the next day prevented. She added, 'Mavra Romano (Matty) *est un ange*, and I cannot love or honour her too much. Your passport to my friendship and affection *is your being her sister!*'

She then threw her rosy fat arms about Matty's neck, and congratulated her (while congratulation was good) on my safety, and promis'd me bushels of friendship, which she anticipated with joy, recommending *herself* to my affection, and kissing me, till my heart was fairly broke, and till I inwardly wish'd that one's friendship was not to be collar'd like a vagabond in that manner whether one was in the humour for it or not. (Don't be afraid for I behaved very decently! and swore horribly in the sacred cause!)

The Princess, (lovely oddity) instantly set about manufacturing a prodigious Russian eulogium (which Matty understood, and told me afterwards) puffing off my qualifications, to such a pitch, that the circle about her were completely mute, and I not comprehending a syllable quietly stroll'd up and down the room with Anna Petrovna, excellent soul, amusing myself with the paintings in fresco against the wall.

Supper was announced, and during the time, the Princess Daschkaw, frequently talk'd to me, in English, and then translated everything into Russ, for the benefit of the Widow, embellishing to a marvellous degree, for I was astonish'd at finding the most commonplace observation of mine receiv'd, by virtue of my Interpreter, with amusement and admiration of countenance on the part of the audience!

These things I mention to give you a perfect notion of the blessed Princess! and tho' she uniformly behaves to us, in this

---

* Madame Nebalsin was the Marie Dmitrievna of Tolstoy's *War and Peace*.

manner, she exacts (from Imperial habits I suppose) a sort of deference, that surprised me excessively at first, from her country people! For example, no man tho' cover'd with Stars attempts to sit down in her presence, without being desired. And this not always being requested, I have seen half a dozen princes stand out an entire visit. Once I saw them *bow'd* out of the room, when she got deadly tired of them and after giving them her hand to kiss they disappear'd!

It never enters into her head or heart to disguise any sentiment or impulse from either, and therefore you may guess what a privileged sort of mortal she makes herself! The truth is sure to come out, whether agreeable or disagreeable, and lucky it is that she has sensibility and gentleness of nature, for if she had not, she wou'd be a public scourge! She is the first by right, rank, sense and habit in every company, and prerogative, becomes such a matter of course, that nothing appears extraordinary that she does.

I mention'd in my last letter the circumstance of her transforming the drawing room into a bedchamber for my accommodation. Well, another thing she did, was to call out at supper for a basket, which she kept on her lap, and stored full of pine apple, peaches, grapes etc. ordering it to be left on her dressing table, and guess what this was for! Because she heard me say I was not fond of fruit except before breakfast, and she would not break through the habit she had establish'd of waking me (by one of her *femmes de chambre*) with this offering, a ceremony she has never omitted a single morning since I came.

I expostulated a little, but the answer I always get on these occasions is

'Rest tranquil my sweet friend! dease 'ittle testimonies *sont les besoins de mon coeur*.' Or else, 'Our younger sister (Matty) must be humour'd. She would scold me if I was not to do my duty.'

In short 'tis endless to detail the hourly marks of her affection and attention not to say adoration for Matty.

Yesterday a tributary Jew or prince or somebody from abroad sent her a new fashion'd long shawl embroider'd in floss yellow silk.

'One must return de favor of ones friend, and he will feel how I honor him for tinking his poor shawl worthy of being accepted by my Angel Child.'

These were her words, when she wound it round Matty's shoulders.

She is planning another picture of Matty. One she wears on her snuff-box, another (as large as life) hangs in her bedchamber here, and a *third* also as large as life (both three quarter'd) is the principal object in her drawing room at Moscow. These (two of them) are elegant looking, and exquisitely dress'd, *none* however strikingly like. Oh, that *abomination* that my Mother has got! Matty has promised me to have a good one copied this winter, and sent home in spring for the drawing room or music room at home, on condition that the other is destroy'd. One of the Princess's persuasions is that Matty is a *perfect beauty*. To doubt this is heresy! And as all the varieties are not expressed in one single picture I have no doubt that before she stops a dozen will be drawn! In fact this is so establish'd an idea that without hazarding an investigation Anna Petrovna and I (neither of whom Lord help us have perform'd any metamorphosis since our birth) take her on the grounds of a Venus de Medicis! I solemnly protest, I do not exaggerate an iota!

You know *my* high opinion of Matty has ever been notorious! You may swear in the extraordinary circumstances under which she came to Russia (and still more into so extraordinary and complicated a family) that her conduct and sense must have play'd a distinguish'd part! These qualities have not lain dormant on any subject whatsoever, at any time. Nor with any branch of the house of Daschkaw, and I have every reason to think, that great as the Princess's partiality is, justice is barely compensated by her devotion, admiration, respect and adulation of *her* character.

I do not speak from partiality, and here comes a proof of handsome conduct on the part of the Princess, which still has had its balance. The Princess sent up a parcel seal'd, and a memorandum on the outside that it contains £3,000.

Here are the words written on the back, in the Princess's hand: 'I beseech you not to open this pacquet but after my death, and then accept the contents, from a friend, a Mother, who *taught* herself under a great obligation to you, and who loved you most tenderly.'

Matty, expostulated, wrote, talk'd, cried, and in short ended by writing these words on the other side: 'If I die before my beloved Princess D. I bequeath this pacquet to her, and in case of her refusing to accept it, I leave it as a testimony of my esteem to the Prince Daschkaw her son. Martha Wilmot.' So ends the affair, and there the pacquet lies in Matty's strong box. This transaction took place 22nd August, the day before they set out to meet me at Moscow.

Since I am on the subject of presents I must mention a gorgeous gold snuff box with the Empress's picture emboss'd which Matty was obliged to accept, a collection of gems in the line of natural history – a collection of coins, a collection of medals, and little *odd come dods* from Herculaneum – two gold lion headed clasps taken from the golden hoards of Tartars (conquer'd many years ago by the Russians and exterminated by John the Terrible), also a full suit of Russian costume worn at court by Princess Daschkaw – agate snuff box – blood stone ditto – a comb – broach – band for the head – necklace, and three rings of torquoise. This set of ornaments are sentimentally arranged in pearls and topas's in a wreath so as to resemble the little flowers call'd *forget me not*. She has also given her a lovely watch (tho' she had one of her own), gold Venetian chains and myriads of seals –a gold comb – a gold and pearl crescent – eighteen different rings – exquisite cornelian earrings like bunches of red currants – pearl necklace and bracelets, beautiful ones – coral ones, – amber ones – a small pianoforte – a beautiful guitar – quantities of music – silver cups – boxes without end, etc. etc.

Then as to cloaths I literally believe she has satin dresses of every colour under the sun, mock lace dresses – a real black lace veil, which covers her from head to foot – velvet dresses – crape ones – muffs – pelices etc. etc. and a library of more than one hundred and fifty valuable books – maps etc. etc. 'Tis all *a chance* when she gets really valuable things, for whether it is a *diamond* or a *flower* I think the Princess seems to know no difference, and would not give it, if she thought there was any other value attached, than what her affection insures.[3]

Meanwhile Katherine's maid, Eleanor Cavanagh, was recording her own impressions; of the journey to Moscow; of life below stairs at the Princess's, and of their subsequent journey to Troitskoe, the Princess's estate sixty miles south of Moscow:

[Troitskoe] October 4th, 1805 [to her father]
We were in a very pleasant carriage the time of coming from Petersburg and travel'd in it for eight days and eight nights too. My mistress brought me blankets and a pillow (the same as her herself) and we had plenty of leather ones, so I'll engage I slept through the night fair enough and stretch'd at my full length because it was *quairly* made on purpose for travelling through the night as well as the day.

Well sure enough we *druve* right into Moscow, and it was the handsomest palace my hand ever seen, like half a round, and a big temple at the top of stone steps!

An army, God knows, might live *unknownst* in the house! This was the Princess Daschkaw's. I'll engage I'll never forget it! I was not two hours there when Miss Matty Wilmot up and she says to me, 'Eleanor,' says she, 'wou'dn't you be afraid of the cold in the country?'

'I don't know ma'am,' says I, 'for all I know about it is very hot!'

With that she laugh'd (Ogh! She is a nice little craiture!) and out she call'd her maid Sophia and talk'd to her in Russian – that I mighten'd stir, but I thought the eyes would have dropt out of my head when I seen the beautifulest cloak that hands ever made put straight upon my shoulders!

'My God!' says I to myself, 'what's all this for! If I was in Glanmire now,' says I, 'the Girls wou'dn't know me!'

"'Tis for you, Eleanor,' says she. 'There Eleanor is the makings of a Sunday gound for you.'

'Is it joking you are Ma'am?' says I.

'No, sure enough I am not joking,' says she, 'but cut it out and make it in to a dress gown for yourself.'

Oh such a nice coat, and such a cloak (pelise they call it in this country) as she clapt on my shoulders! 'Tis a twill'd purple and brown silk lined all thro' and through with snow white fur and trimm'd at the edge with fur. The worth of it is five guineas.

Sophia (Miss Matty's maid) indeed is a very good natured and pretty girl.

'Eleanor,' she says to me from the first minute and kiss'd both my cheeks just as if she doated down upon me.

'I never seen you before to my knowledge,' said I.

'How do you do,' (as naturally as anything) says a smart little girl about eleven years old.

'I'm very well,' says I.

'That's *Martishka* (says Miss Matty), another girl belonging to me and who I am bringing up myself. So Eleanor,' says she, "'tis for you to shew her a good example.'

'That's true Ma'am,' says I.

The girls then took me in to supper. It was near eleven o'clock. Plenty of fish and nice hashes and pies and grapes and apples and water melon. They were all very merry and making me eat and drink. 'Twas they who had the grand earrings in their ears and without any caps at all on their heads.

'Twas hard for me to swallow a mouthful with all the pictures looking at me, some of them *without a tack* upon their backs except wings like birds upon their shoulders.

But it wasn't them I was thinking of, 'twas the Princess of the Palace, Princess Daschkaw that I heard talk of so much in Ireland and all through Russia! I look'd everywhere and down over the bannisters when we were coming up stairs to bed! But tho' I seen plenty of people I could not make her off at all.

Just before my mistress went into her room, bounce! the door open'd and in walk'd the Princess with a large Star upon her breast and as good a face smiling and looking as good natured as a child! She did not see me at first at all, but it came into my head she had just the look of Mrs Chetwood the day she gave me the white wine up at the house for you.

She staid some time, and the minute she spied me out (for I kept standing at the bedroom door) she took me by the hand, and,

'I'm glad to see you,' says she, and kiss'd me as kind as if I had belong'd to her.

'I'm oblig'd to you Ma'am,' says I, and turn'd as red as a rose.

'Ellen,' says she, 'are you alive after the journey?'

'Faith I am Ma'am,' says I. ('What would kill me?' thought I, but I did not say so out loud.) May I never stir but she is the pleasantest Lady I ever seen in or out of Ireland! The next morning she give me my choice of three of the handsomest shawls as big as quilts, and I chose one, a purple in the inside and a scarlet border. Up I put it on my back and made a curtsey *as stiff as two pence!*

The next evening the Princess sent her maids and Miss Matty's maids and myself to the finest play house the world ever seen, and by the same token I wore my shawl and we all walk'd there very pleasantly. I turn'd round my head and as grand as nothing at all there I seen a man servant walking behind us.

'Faith,' says I, "tis very droll! Walk slow,' says I to Nastasia (the Princess's first maid), 'don't you see the man is not come up with us yet.' With that she shook her head and on we went to the play house.

The life almost dropt out of me when the curtain was drawn up. There we were all sitting in the pit, and taken care of I'll be bound, for a guard stood all the time and walk'd home with us to the palace besides the servant. The play was like Heaven himself. There was a dragon! and kings! and birds! and a witch! and loads of music! and flames, and ladies and gentlemen in gold and diamonds dancing, not on the ground at all hardly, and the beautiful noise! and smoke! and plenty of pleasure of all kinds!

127

'Ogh!' says I, clapping my hands, 'Mary Nugent and Kiff wou'dn't believe the sight I seen.' With that I look'd up and thought I was in the air with the Angels.

From Moscow to the country palace where we now are and where we have been three weeks is more than eighty-six mile. 'Twas like an army when we left Moscow! Such loads of coaches and sarvants! I *druve* with the Princess's first maid Nastasia. At night the devil an inn we came to, but a big palace belonging to a Count!

We all sat very warm and pleasant, and then a sight of maids belonging to the palace came in and kiss'd us all round. I counted eleven of them, handsome looking girls enough, and mighty civil and nice. They made signs to us and we all follow'd them out of doors across a garden to a *darling* place, and up we went up stairs (Sophia and I with our hands under one another's arms) till we got into a play house. *May I never stir* but I believe it was! There was an auld man with a trumpet in his mouth and his two eyes looking at me.

'Come here,' says Miss Anna Petrovna, the Princess neice (a fine young lady who lives with her always). 'Come here,' says she.

'I'm frighten'd Ma'am,' says I.

Ogh then, such things as I seen nobody knows but my own self! I look'd thro' a little hole, and faith there I seen London and Petersburg and cart loads of grand towns, but 'twas very *quair* Cork did not come any how!

There was voices of live people talking out of little small trumpets and singing, and doing everything like Christians.

'Well to be sure,' says I. 'Russia! and good luck to you, you are a comical place! and you'll give me something to talk of many a long day!'

But this is not all, for when we went back to the palace again there were twenty musicians with fiddles and flutes and all sorts of music playing *as fine as five pence*!

'Carry me out!' says I. 'What will come next?'

As sure as I am a gun I guess'd right enough, for then people came in and danc'd and sung all the time the company was eating their suppers, and they did not hinder us from standing at the door to listen and look at all the fun.

When supper was over I took notice that the Princess cross'd and bless'd herself and went away into another room and all the rest follow'd. So without more ado down all of us sat to the same table and the men servants attended us, and I believe there was more than one hundred dishes, fruit too of the finest sorts and kinds.

We slept there and the next morning we were up by six , and when the ladies drank their cups of coffee I thought we were going off with ourselves, when my nose told my heart more dinner was coming. And sure enough tho' it was early there was smoking dishes of meat and fish and pies and fruit and wine just as if it was four o'clock. And when the quality had finish'd no blam'st to us all eighteen maid sarvents if we did not eat our belly fulls! The laugh was not out of my mouth all the time, everything was so jolly and pleasant in itself.

That night we slept at an inn belonging to the Princess herself, and the day after we came to where we are now, a grand elegant place, handsomer than Mr Courtney's up at Lota! The name it goes by is Troitskoe. That is as much as to say *Trinity* in Russian, God save us!

The first thing the Princess done was to go to the chapel, a beautiful one she has of her own, and the priests gave her the crucifix to kiss and sung psalms and burnt the blessed ashes, and then two men at the pillars of the gate leading into the lawn *stud* with a great loaf of black bread and a handful of salt on the top of it, and the princess receiv'd it as an offering, and gave them her hand to kiss. And everyone was running to welcome her home tho' she had been only away a couple of weeks. . . .

There is ten villages all belonging to the Princess here, and them that lives in them comes to the number of three thousand men and women, all her subjects and loving her as if she was their mother. There is two hundred servants that lives in and out of the house.

129

She one morning sent for me, and she was sitting in her own room about seven o'clock in the morning.

'Ellen,' says she, 'I believe you have none of the money of my country.'

'No Ma'am,' says I.

'Well then,' says she (looking as good humour'd as anything), 'you ought to know how to reckon, and so here are twenty roubles for you (each rouble is more than half a crown), and they are in different kinds of coin, you will learn to understand the value.'

'Ma'am,' says I, 'I'm very much oblig'd to you,' and with that I kiss'd her hand.

Oh I forgot to tell you that she put the money into a blue purse work'd with gold and tied with white ribbon and five gold tassels. I never seen such a purse, nor anything so handsome in my life! . . .

There is not a Sunday morning that my mistress don't ask me if I have been to prayers, and she would not be pleased at all if I miss them. Once besides in the week I went, for there is many and many a holy day kept here. . . .

We'll all be *laiving* this the 13th of December for Moscow again where we are to stay three months in the same palace of the Princess I talk'd to you about. And God knows I never seen such a good lady since ever I was born, nor so kind, nor so generous I've reason to say dear knows! Once every week there is a play acted here in a nice little play house belonging to the Princess. We are all given *laive* to go. 'Tis the sarvents who act just for her amusement. . . .

The weather is not a bit colder yet a while and the stoves make the halls and rooms much warmer than fires. They are lit once a day. We breakfast early and then dine at the Princess's own table as soon as the ladies and gentlemen go into the drawing room. 'Tis wonderful how early they dine, always between one and two o'clock, so that the girls and myself sits down at four, but none of the men sarvents, and I'll engage we live like Queens! 'Tis the same at supper, for we have one like a hot dinner at ten o'clock afterwards. . . .

130

Once at Troitskoe, the sisters settled into the routine the Princess loved, but which Katherine initially found tedious, since much of her normal day was spent in writing.

September 24th Troitskoe [1805] [to her sister-in-law Anna Chetwood]

We assemble at nine in the morning to drink our coffee attended by *filles de chambres*, and then what with lounging or talking or music or walking, most frequently a couple of hours are spent, Lord knows how! Then instead of picking up lost time, from that till five o'clock, the thunder of the dinner bell (like the death signal to all occupation and leisure) sounds at half past one or two at farthest, and we assemble to solemnize our long repast, where each several dish, of two courses, and a dessert, are not only carved on another table and handed to you, but you are expected to eat of them all without mercy.

This is one of the Princess's particularities. Everything is better dress'd and done, than anywhere! and she prides herself on the produce of her farm, dairy, gardens, hot houses, pineries, etc. etc. I have acquired a passion for the drink of this country (call'd quass)* which is intolerable everywhere but here, but which I like better than champaigne. Honey with fresh cucumbers is a favorite dish, preserved dates, and apple bread, young pig and cold cream, egg paties eat with soup, another soup made of fish, and every sort of sallad and eat cold. In fact there is no end to the whimsical varieties that a Russian kitchen furnishes peculiar to itself, together with imitations from every other in the world.

But to return to the disposition of time. Dinner breaks in compleatly upon the day, and 'tis difficult to return to one's morning's avocations. Tea then assembles the family again at six o'clock, and a prodigious hot supper at half past nine or ten. Well, it can't be help'd! . . .

---

* A drink fermented from a mixture of rye-flour with malt. Likened to penny ale.

In fact Katherine was not well, had little appetite, and no energy. For a time Matty thought this must be due to the change of air, it was only when her sister turned bright yellow that everyone realized she had jaundice.

'I'm sure she has long had a heavy lodgment of bile which probably the sea stirred up,' Matty wrote to their mother by way of explanation, 'tho' it did not dissipate it for her as it did for Ellen* who is now as fresh as a rose and as merry as a cricket, which I wish you would tell her father and brother, as well as her mistress's approbation of her conduct. It is really incredible how cleverly she makes herself understood amongst the servants and carries her point thro' thick and thin.'[4]

In spite of her jaundice Katherine was becoming fascinated by Troitskoe.

Octr 1st [1805]

What will I be after saying to you? I believe I never mention'd Troitska. It is a fine place, the Princess has made it herself, and situated it in the midst of sixteen villages belonging to her. Three thousand peasants, 'My subjects' (as she calls them), live most happily under her absolute power. And of all the blessed hearted beings that ever existed on that subject she is the most blessed (excepting your Mother).

There are two hundred servants, taking in all denominations inside and outside, in this establishment, more than a hundred horses, two hundred stock of cows, and everything else in proportion. The church establishment too belongs to her, and is built at the back of the house. A lovely wood belonging to the estate nine miles long and four broad is within a few yards of the place (inhabited by wolves) and in it the Princess and I lost our way yesterday evening for an hour and half.

A beautiful river winds all through the grounds and serpentines amidst the entire estate. However Troitska is a dead flat (almost) and to the cultivation alone its beauty is attributable. An immense quantity of ground is laid out under shrubberies and

---

* Eleanor.

all sorts of pleasure grounds completely in the English stile. The house is enormous with wings on either side which are only connected by balconies raised on iron railings up to the second story. Matty and I inhabit one of these wings and Anna Petrovna the other. Twenty bearded men are now busily employ'd in making a temporary wooden passage from the hall door to the door of our castle, as in winter (strange to say) they had provided for no internal communication so much was sacrificed to the appearance of the outside. . . .

In the midst of this immense establishment and in the center of riches and honours I wish you were to see the Princess go out to take a walk, or rather to look over her subjects! An old brown great coat and a silk pocket handkerchief about her neck, *worn to rags* is her dress, and well may it be worn to rags for she has worn it eighteen years and will continue to do so as long as she lives because it belong'd to Mrs Hamilton.*

Her originality, her appearance, her manner of speaking, her doing every description of thing, (for she helps the masons to build walls, she assists with her own hands in making the roads, she feeds the cows, she composes music, she sings and plays, she writes for the press, she shells the corn, she talks out loud in church and corrects the priest if he is not devout, she talks out loud in her little theatre and puts in the performers when they are out in their parts, she is a doctor, an apothecary, a surgeon, a farrier, a carpenter, a magistrate, a lawyer. In short she hourly practices every species of incongruity, corresponds with her brother† (who holds the first post in the Empire) on his trade, with authors, with philosophers, with Jews, with poets, with her son, with all her relations, and yet appears as if she had her time a burthen on her hands) altogether gives me eternally the idea of her being a Fairy! And I protest it is not jokingly I say so, for the impression never quits me for a moment.

---

* A cousin of Katherine and Martha's father.

† Count Alexander Romanovich Woronzow (1741–1805). Russian Imperial Chancellor.

The marvellous contradiction too of her speaking like an infant in her broken English and with her unaccountable expressions! She is unconscious whether she speaks French, English or Russian, and mingles these in every sentence. She speaks German and Italien equally well, but her pronunciation is not clear which takes from the pleasure I shou'd otherwise receive from her conversation.

I have just finish'd reading Voltaire's, Diderot's, Garrick's and the Abbé Raynall's letters to her. She has promised me the Empress Catherine's, and I have also read a good part of her life* written by herself.

Indeed it is necessary to qualify oneself with the knowledge of public things and characters in Russia since the time of Catherine, since the Princess alludes to them perpetually and her mind wanders so naturally back to the court and study and toilet and boudoir of Catherine, that I am beginning to fancy I recollect her habits of life and conversation, and that *I* was a party concern'd in the revolution.

By the by, the principal reception room at Troitska is orna- mented with an immense picture of Catherine on horseback in uniform taken the very day of her husband's destruction, and the Princess says a *perfect* resemblance. Besides this there are portraits of her in every room.

Yesterday morning when I went down to breakfast I saw the Princess fuming over the herring which she was preparing for me to swallow, as I had been heard to complain in the secret recesses of my castle of an uncomfortable feel in my stomach, and the Fairy knew it by inspiration and did cause a fish to rise from its troubled waters and dissipate, perforce of magic, my derangement!

I happen'd to come down before Matty, and the flash of terror that appear'd in her eyes, frighten'd me out of my wits for a moment. On enquiry it proved to be her anguish at the notion of

---

* Her famous *Memoirs* which Matty had persuaded her to write.

Matty's perhaps being unwell, and her expression was, *'de taught cut my heart like a sharp knife'*. . . .

October 2nd [1805]
. . . hang me if I put pen to paper again while I remain at Troitska, excepting to announce my *petrefaction* if it takes place according to promise. *Petrefaction* brings hot water into my head and this reminds me of the bath establishment in the shrubbery here which is lovely and most perfectly arranged. The women have nothing else to do but to heat the furnace and keep everything in order, and you know bathing is with the Russians as with the Turks a religious observance as not one of the lower order would or could profane the church without having been in the hot bath the night before. This secures a universal ablution every Saturday regularly.

The bath here has three seperate chambers. In one is a gradation of stairs to increase the heat of a vapour bath if you like it. There is also a great tub in which one sits up to the chin and the ceremony is to scour oneself with horse-reddish till you smart and then with soap. You should first sit up to your knees in a composition of wormwood, nettles, grass-seed, mint, and horsereddish. I have gone through this operation frequently. The Princess always goes to bed which is prepared in an adjoining chamber, but I go walk about and only feel the stronger.

The Princess, sweet woman, has promised me (laughing most heartily at the thoughts of what with any one else would be nothing and yet from her methodical and clockwork habits of life is a real sacrifice) to leave Troitska *two days* sooner than she ever did before in order to go to Moscow and shew me the lions.

She says Count Alexis Orloff shall give a ball – on these occasions she sends her order and the ball is given as a matter of allegiance. She has also promised that concerts shall be given at her house. She promises too to take me to the Kremlin and order the Archbishop of Georgia to prepare a feast for the occasion. The Kremlin you know is in the middle of the town of Moscow, a town in itself containing all the religion of the Empire.

135

To be sure there never were strangers more capitally circumstanced for seeing all that is to be seen than we are. I am longing to go to Moscow. Amongst other things she wanted to take me into Poland in spring, but this I sturdily refused, as travelling is dangerous for her internal disorders which are of the most dangerous nature. This I knew and wrote to her from St Petersburg, to intreat she would not leave Troitska on my account, but nothing could stop her nor no selfish consideration impede for one moment her resolution of giving me the reception she had design'd.

Don't irritate me by saying you suppose I am beginning to speak the language. No! Let that satisfy you for ever. I feel my power of *Duncishness* increase daily! My powers of idleness! My powers of hopelessness on everything that's good! So God be with you. Not so Matty. She reads, writes and speaks Russ wonderfully. The Princess teaches her, and they correspond in notes every day almost.

I must fly! I see the Fairy beckoning me with her wand! and nobody knows what necromancy she is after! . . .

Troitskoe. December 2nd 1805 [to her sister Alicia]
I told you I believe that Troitskoe was circumstanc'd like a sprig of lily of the valley, that is the white stucco'd house is shaded with a dark spreading forest of seven miles breadth. Into this we regularly penetrate on our sledges drawn by three horses abreast full speed, surging us through the snow, (like a boat breaking through the waves) and sending up a sparkling spray which makes us move in an atmosphere of diamonds. . . .

The solitude of this forest, (which in the night is broken sometimes by the marauding of the wolves) is seldom interrupted in *our* course, excepting by wood cutters who look like *satyrs* rather than human beings, and whose endless beards (clogg'd in snow and lengthen'd by icicles) crackle in responsive measure to their hatchets' strokes. . . .

You perceive here we drive in by the back of the house that wide range of buildings, (which hems in the lawn circularly and in the midst of which the church stands) must be accounted for as appurtenances to the castle, or else you might mistake it for a little town. One is a theatre – another a riding school – a third an infirmary – a fourth the stables – a fifth the steward's house – a sixth a house for guests – a seventh a house for a gigantic English bull – an eighth, ninth, tenth, eleventh for servants and so on.

Mercy on us. What a wilderness of a looking hall here is! No wonder it should be so when it is the eternal passage of such a swarm of servants! You must let that triangular looking Stepousha, (blinking behind his cravat) help you off with your mufflements, while Affanasia takes off your fur boots, and while Vinsens, Masayee, Kusma, Bessilkin, Vassilee, Kashan, Prokev, Antoine, Timothée and half a score others of different shapes and colours, run to usher you into the dining room (exactly opposite the hall door) and so from the left of the dining parlour into the usual sitting room. The furniture of this room is red morocco leather and gold. You perceive 'tis the shape of the music room at home on a larger scale.

That portrait at the head of the room hanging over the sopha is Princess Daschkaw's husband, who was reckon'd the beauty of his time and who died when he was only six and twenty years of age!* That commanding looking dame with eagles embroider'd on her train and an ermine robe is Catherine II of Russia, and opposite is her grandson Alexander I in all his Imperial dignity. So far for pictures.

At the upper end of the room sitting in an arm chair, with a little table before her (inlaid like a chess board) lounging in purple silk dressing gown, and white man's nightcap, with her black dog Fidelle, sleeping on a cushion at her feet, is the Princess! She is waiting for our return home, as this evening is to be dedicated to reading over some dozen letters, she has tied up in that great paper parcel! – the successive correspondence, that pass'd between her and Catherine II from the time she was eighteen years of age till she resign'd the Academy. These

---

* Prince Kodrat (Michael) Dashkov (1736–64).

subjects (as ripping up a life that is almost past) gives a painful sort of agitated animation to her countenance, and I long till it is over. Anna Petrovna has already taken up her station and prepared her great worsted knitting. . . .

Sunday. Decr. 7th [1805]
You perceive five days have pass'd since I was interrupted, and till this morning that suddenly this sheet of paper fell out of my desk in a general crash I totally forgot it was in existence. Within this time Saint Katherine, the patron saint of Princess Daschkaw, has walk'd in amongst us to gather her taxes and exact her perquisites both temporal and spiritual.

The Princess and I being name sakes she was resolved this fête should be doubly celebrated, and therefore the eve of the day a solemn Mass was held for the beatification of our souls.

This was thursday evening and in the dining hall the priests and chaunters were all assembled with the incense and images . . . the silver Image of Saint Katherine blaz'd before the glass with her tributary lights.

After this ceremony was ended everybody of every description press'd forward to offer their congratulations and presents. Peasants in tribes lined the hall, each with a large loaf of bread cover'd over with a heap of salt which they offer'd as their homage and some a little plate of apples to enhance the tribute. After this the Princess and I exchanged presents and both receiv'd those of Anna Petrovna and Matty.

The Princess's offering to me was *most exquisite*, it was a mosaic snuff box set in gold, the lid bearing in mosaic colouring the famous Roman pyramid of Caius Cestus . . . this accompanied by a letter, which I shall transcribe verbatim –

I don't want to lead you by the nose – besides I know I couldn't – but it is to delight one of your senses, that I am giving you this little snuff-box.

St Catherine, who is the patron saint of both of us, told me that on her feast day it was to *you* I should make an offering in

138

order to please *her* – and I quickly decided to do this as delicately as I could. Pondering what was best, I decided that it was through the five senses that we experienced pleasure or the reverse. Convinced that I was no longer beautiful to look at! that to touch I was no more than a skeleton, to hear, but an exhumed Orpheus, and that your taste neither could nor would have any of me – there was left to me solely the sense of smell.

Allow me then, my darling friend, to make an offering to this sense, which most nearly makes up for my inability to fulfill the commands of our Patron. I shall then be able to make my peace with her. . . .[5]

My offering to her was a large quilted green silk pocket book, to write her memorandums in – and the first page scrawl'd with the following garbage:

> As motionless and snowy as this page
> Pigmalion's work had shared oblivion's dower
> But that a kindling ray of roseate light
> Woke it to thrilling life, with quickening power.
> So will this little Book! (now marble white)
> If to its leaves one thought is e'er consign'd,
> Vibrate th'inspiring impulse, Virtue gives,
> And live – the Heavenly record of Your Mind.
>
> K. WILMOT

. . . I don't believe I ever walk'd you up stairs! Whisk the tail of your gown then, again, over your shoulders and ascend these stone stairs. At the top of the second flight turn to your left into the antechamber. Those are all the old pictures of the house of Daschkaw and Worontzow. Now enter into the drawing room, or rather public looking ball room, for it is really magnificent. What a picture is that of Catherine ii on a grey horse dress'd in the uniform of the Guards as large as life, as she appear'd the famous 28th of June 1762, the day of the Russian Revolution! Reflected in the opposite looking glass it appears galloping

139

towards you, as your movement gives it motion. That to the left is the King of Prussia, her contemporary, and that again the unfortunate Stanislaus King of Poland.

The floors are all inlaid, with different coloured wood, as is most of the furniture. Now pass into the second drawing room, 'tis lovely! Only think of this extraordinary Princess, not only having plann'd the house herself, but having assisted the masons to build it *with her own hands*. Never mind the suite of rooms which follow, they are only bedchambers. But 'tis worth while going up stairs again to the library which contains God knows how many thousand volumes, in half a dozen different languages. The room commands a view of all the encircling country, and is supported by pillars, each of which, is in itself a little library. Up stairs again is the apothecary's hall etc. etc.

There you are then in the chimney (like a dwarf in a marrow bone) and there you may stay with the million of crows which are eternally flying about the roof of this house. . . .

Monday December 8th [1805]
I protest your *cawing* has woke me this morning out of my slumbers! Can't you spend a night on the roof of a house without making such an uproar? Come down stairs then into the garden, or rather shrubbery which is very pleasant to walk in as the walks are swept every day and the snow does not incommode one in the least. Besides if you feel it cold we can walk in the Orangerie.

That winding walk among the birch trees is a favourite one of the Princess because of its leading to the monument of granite erected on a mount and dedicated to the remembrance of the day Catherine ascended the throne! Behind it is scoop'd a Hermit's cell furnish'd with moss and rocky seats out of which you plunge into the depth of a wood! But what nonsense to talk of woods and cells and winding walks in this weather – you had better return with me to my own room where I always breakfast and from whence I never descend untill one or two o'clock to dinner. . . .

Have you a fancy to eat your dinner? . . . Run down stairs then and take your seat at the great square board. You must first eat egg pâtés with your soup and then drink hydromel* to wash them down or else quass. With your roasted meat you must eat salt cucumbers, and then caviare made of the roe of sturgeon. Young pig and curdled cream is at your service next, and *lachat* which is the general name for all grain baked with cream. Fish soup do you chuse? Fowls? Game? Vegetables? or apple bread? or raw apples from the Crimea? or the Siberian apples? or the transparent apples? or the Kieff sweetmeat? or honey comb? or preserved rose leaves, or pickled plums?

In the name of God eat no more! For in six or seven hours, you will have to sit down to just such another dinner under the name of supper! So (unless you go away with yourself) you must, while they are perfuming the rooms, which suffocates me, wander down the long passage into the Princess's cabinet, sweet old woman that she is!

So I may say at least, and as for Matty, there's no talking on that subject! The affectionate distinction and animated cordiality, which has accompanied every word and action towards me ever since I first saw her, has never had one moment's interruption. She calls me the sister of her choice, and, added to the playfulness of her countenance and manner, whenever she addresses me, her ingenuity appears restless to search for circumstances to commend and flatter, in everything touching myself, my family, or my country.

Tho' I do her but common justice in mentioning these things, yet trust me, I feel *myself* very little involv'd in the main spring of her conduct. For being Matty's sister, is in her eyes *everything* to irradiate humanity into the beatification of a ministering angel of light. Sometimes she exclaims with devotion when she looks at her:

'Dare is de mark of Heaven's best love to me. My darling child sought me out on the credit of my name, and came by herself

---

* A concoction of honey and water.

141

from distant country, in de faith of my character! Now do tell me sister Kaightty what shall I ever do to prove my love and gratitude to her?'

Regularly every three or four days I am told the story over and over again with renew'd energy. Perhaps you don't know that I mean my own name by spelling it as she pronounces it in her broken English 'Sister Kaightty', but the drollery this gives her conversation is inexpressible. I was call'd into her cabinet the other day to read the dedication she had just finished to Matty of her History.* It is written most elegantly, and the natural affection, admiration, gratitude, and enthusiasm it breathes towards Matty certainly is the most noble testimonial that it is possible for one individual to pay another.

I have, since I came here, often thought what a task it would be to attempt to draw the character of the Princess Daschkaw! . . . she has as many climates to her mind, as many splinters of insulation, as many oceans of agitated uncertainty, as many Etnas of destructive fire, and as many wild wastes of blighted cultivation as exists in any quarter of the globe! For my part I think she would be most in her element at the *Helm of the State*, or Generalissimo of the army, or Farmer General of the Empire. In fact she was born for business on a large scale which is not irreconcilable with the life of a woman who at eighteen headed a revolution and who for twelve years afterwards govern'd an Academy of Arts & Sciences. . . .

You will never believe me when I say the Princess has no sense of the ridiculous. I don't think she comprehends a caricature even in language. A little instance pass'd yesterday at dinner. She told Matty it was a shame for her not to take snuff as she had seven or eight Imperial boxes, and jokingly ask'd me what punishment she should inflict! Anna Petrovna and I profoundly suggested that the Princess should serve Matty's nose as she does her favourite trees in the shrubbery – crop it till as many noses sprang up in a copse as she had gorgeous snuff

* The Princess's *Memoirs*.

142

boxes. The Princess look'd ready to cry, and thought us no better than butchers. She instantly turn'd the conversation.

15 December 1805 – 21 October 1806

Saturday Night. Moscow. December 15th [1805]
We are just arriv'd here after the most dreadful journey ever made, but our joy in finding ourselves in Moscow is sadly alloy'd by the news which has just reach'd the Princess, namely that her favorite brother, the Grand Chancellor, is not expected to live.* . . . This is a dreadful shock!

I must go to bed, my bones being in a jelly after the roads which were broken and of course in hills and vallies of ice!

Moscow. 18th Feby 1806 [to her sister Alicia]
I'll talk of dinner now and not of your letter which robb'd me of mine, as a Christian return for which I will give you the offering of twenty-seven feasts, that being the number of dinnerings we have figured at since the 6th of January, Christmas day here.

As you may conclude, I feel a little tired with them. Their luxuries and magnificence soon lose their effect, and the unnatural hours kept here totally destroy every species of pleasure when once the gloss of novelty is at an end.

The effect left upon my imagination is that of having flitted amongst the ghosts of the Court of Catherine. Moscow is the Imperial, terrestrial, political Elysium of Russia. All those placemen whose power existed in the reign of Catherine and of Paul, and all those discarded or conceiv'd superannuated by Alexander, hold an *ideal* consequence (awarded by courtesy alone) in this lazy idle magnificent and Asiatic town. For all the effective power has long since pass'd as an inheritance to their successors, who rule the Imperial realm at Petersburg, and flatter away their hours about the Court.

* Count Alexander Woronzow.

144

Nevertheless the ruffled, decorated phantom of Prince Gallitzen, (Grand Chamberlain in the time of Catherine) retains its orders, its stars and its ribbons, which added to the weight of four score years and ten, bends it double to the ground. It wears its key of diamonds, its bag and embroidery and all its glittering baubles, on its *bones*, and receives the homage of its brother ghosts, who in former days shared with him the honors of state.

Another of these gaudy phantoms is Count Ostrowman, Grand Chancellor of the Empire in the reign of Catherine. The orders of St George, of St Alexander Neffsky, St Wolodimer etc. etc. hang it over in red, blue, and different coloured stripes. Eighty-three years have frozen in a pyramid upon his head, and his gibbering skeleton rattles in his coach and eight, with out riders, dines with his high Dukes behind his chair, and in fact enacts the same etiquette from courtesy that was awarded him in his more effective days of Imperial favor.

Count Alexis Orloff, who was Grand Admiral in the time of Catherine, is richer than any Prince in Christendom, and revels in Asiatic luxury. The hand that strangled Peter,* is cover'd with its recompence of brilliants, beneath which the portrait of Catherine smiles in eternal gratitude. . . . I confess I am heartily sick of the name of *Great Catherine* by this group of displaced place dotards. She is praised uniformly with a reference to *their own Services*, and what is really doing in Russia in the political world, I don't know. As uniformly Alexander† is esteem'd a driveller, a Frenchified innovator, a schoolboy, and a tyrant in embryo; and since they themselves have quitted the helm of public affairs, the vessel has been they think, toss'd in a hurricane of error and impending misfortune. . . .

One general observation I have made, is that in their comparison of the English and French, the Moscovites (and I fancy I might say the Russians) prejudices are all in favour of the

* Peter iii of Russia (1728–62), Catherine's husband, assassinated in a palace revolution in 1762.
† The Emperor Alexander i (1777–1825).

latter practically speaking. For example, everything is shocking for dinner that is not dress'd by a French cook. Every boy and girl *awkward* who are not educated by French people. Every dress inelegant that is not Parisien etc. etc. . . . Tho' this is all true, and tho' French novels are exclusively *gobbled* by every boy and girl in Moscow, yet there is no one who does not blaspheme against Buonaparte and lament Lord Nelson! The English nation abstractedly is respected, but its practices are unknown, its language rarely spoken, its fashions disliked, and the individuals criticized in a manner absolutely different from any others. Those Englishmen, (travellers) who *are* admired, get credit for what is unusual in their country, such as waltzing well! speaking German, and Russ! calling everyone 'Your Highness' and 'Your Excellency' at every word, and complimenting without mercy everything Russian in spite of the preference they themselves give to French practices! . . . to use Princess Daschkaw's expression upon this subject, 'I do tink God Almighty himself ought to be proud when he says, I have made de English woman.' She is not, however, half so fond of English *men*. . . .

The Princess plays cards constantly – sometimes Faro, sometimes Boston, and sometimes Whist – and hundreds of guineas are lost and won, in constant fluctuation every evening.

This is stupid to Anna Petrovna, Matty and me, and often we accompany either a niece of the Princess, or the Governor's wife to balls, concerts, and plays as (excepting to dinners) the Princess does not go out this winter on account of her brother's death. . . .

Alas! Our sand is nearly run at Moscow, which I am grievously sorry for. It is warmer than at Troitskoe, as a proof of which, I have never sneezed since I came here, nor felt what cold was, thanks to stoves, and mufflements, besides it has been unnaturally mild this winter, and scarcely a day has pass'd that Matty and I have not trudged round the house in the snow, for an hour, (to the amazement of the Russians, who literally never put their feet to the ground) in consequence of which, Matty is twenty times better in health, than she was last winter.

I saw a most curious sight about three weeks ago. I was deploring to the Princess the circumstance of my losing many nationalities from moving too high in the circle of society and saying to her how much I should like to see merchants, and taverns and shopkeepers etc. etc. etc. She most good naturedly promised I should be gratified, and a day was appointed for a party of sixteen or seventeen of us to do dine at the most famous tavern in Moscow.

Everything was compleatly in the Russian stile, every dish peculiar to the country! and I suppose there was at least one hundred of them! To make the matter compleat la Maitress d'Hotel, dress'd in gold embroidery and diamonds, sat at the head of the table with her face, neck and arms painted like a doll.

This painting is not from necessity, but national usage ever since Russia was in existence. Our attendants, to the number of forty, were bearded men dress'd in yellow, purple and various colour'd shirts push'd up at the wrists, so as to leave half their arms naked without coats or waistcoats.

There was a boy who play'd on an organ, and who paid the master of the tavern simply for this permission nine hundred guineas a year, which was but the overplus of his earnings, which shews the concourse of people who daily frequent that place, and look upon music as a necessary of life.

After dinner, coffee, desert, etc. we saw a group of gipseys who were brought in for our diversion. They were dress'd in gold brocaded shawls tied on one shoulder, and earrings form'd of various coins. Oh, how beautifully they danc'd the Bohemian and Egyptian dances! They look'd exactly like the dancing figures found in Herculaneum and Pompeia. Their vivacity border'd on frenzy at some moments, when fear was to be express'd, and their movements, accompanied by abrupt cries, gave so wild and preternatural an effect, that it was impossible to imagine them the inhabitants of this drowsy planet. . . .

Look at the seal of this letter. Yesterday the Princess gave it to me. The Seven Stars, or Great Bear of the North is herself, and the flame on the altar, the sentiment she has lit up in me, which is engraved upon the edge, it is a beautiful seal cut on a precious stone. The Princess has been very unwell and nervous, but is now well again, I have a dismal headache from sitting up half the night at a ball. . . .[1]

They set off from Moscow on Tuesday 17 March. 'The storm and tempest of to-day is terrific,' Matty had written to her mother on the 13th, 'wind whistling in every chink, and the snow driven in whirling collums, and then in drifts all thro' the air.'[2]

The Princess and Matty went ahead, Katherine and Anna Petrovna following. They had no sooner 'flourished out of Moscow in triumph', than the postillions 'plumped them abruptly into a hole in the Ice', 'with such violence', Katherine wrote, that 'frowns and tears! crossings and liquores! sorrows and packages! saints and Russian lamentations! sliced tongues! sighs! cakes! hartshorn! and lap dogs, all emblended in one crash!'[3]

They eventually reached Troitskoe however . . .

Troitskoe. 21st March N.S. 1806 [to Anna Chetwood]
Heavens, eloquent must that expression be which could attempt to convey the suffering of a Russian journey! From the constant passage of merchandise on the roads, they are plough'd up into rocks of frozen and refrozen snow, over which you must drive, instantly flumping down into a proportionable cavity. In these dreadful holes, one is sometimes rooted for twenty minutes at a time, the miserable horses, falling with the exertion of pulling one out, and lashed up again and again by dozens of people and servants, who aid in supporting either side of the carriage.

Besides the coach (in which Anna Petrovna and I had the misfortune of being cramm'd with pillows and writing-cases and one of the dogs) there were eight other conveyances! So that Tuesday morning, when they were all drawn up in a half moon before the door at Moscow, we wanted only a few elephants to give us the appearance of an Indian Army! But added to our corporal sufferings, our buffets and bruises, our sickness and intolerable fatigue, we were in no humour for quitting Moscow at least for six weeks to come.

I speak of A.P.,* Matty and myself, for as to the Princess, she was only suppressing the radience of her joy, never desiring to quit Troitskoe as long as she lives and making her yearly visit to Moscow a sacrifice to others. . . .

We found Matty stretch'd in state upon the sopha, she having arriv'd with the Princess before us, in all the solemnities of indisposition. She had got a violent sore throat and the house was ransacking for remedies!

She has been in bed ever since tho' now perfectly well, and scarcely a moment has that excellent Princess stir'd an inch from her side, except when she help'd to smooth the bed with her own hands, to mix her drink, and to apply cataplasms† to her feet! It was with the most earnest entreaties we could prevent her sitting up all night (after such a journey too), and literally her agonized attention and anxiety has made the service of a *femme de chambre*, almost superfluous.

One of her expressions was,

'*Écoutez, ma chère* Katey, dis day my Jews in Poland *m'ont envoyé* deir rents, two towsand guineas; and I wou'd fling it in de bottom of de river if *dat* wou'd make well my little Angel!'

Another time, Matty told her not to forget that her illness was infectious:

'Well, and what is dat to me! Only *un motive encore plus fort*, for I might take it off upon my own self. I have asked God Almighty dat prayer already.'

Her adoration of her surpasses anything I ever saw – her sentiments might dignify blank verse on this subject, tho' I let them go *in her own words*, which are an eternal source of amusement to me.

What adds to her *naïveté* is the earnestness of countenance and manner, which accompanies all she says and does. Speaking to me just now of this place, which she adores, (after

* Anna Petrovna.
† Poultices.

scrubbing the windows with the skirt of her great coat to get a glimpse of the view) she exclaim'd:

'Now I pray you, dear sister Katey, admire with me my beautiful Troitska. Look, have you seen or in Italy or in France (*mais c'est un très vilain pays*) *même en Angleterre* a ting so perfect, or so magnificent, as *cette superbe prairie a l'autre côté de la rivière*? Tell me out true, is it not *un vrai Paradis?*'

'Indeed Princess I see nothing but snow. It was very green and pretty last October, but I can discern nothing, absolutely nothing of what you speak.'

'*Cependant, ma chère amie, avec votre esprit* you might give de seasons changing upon de earth! *Passons le dessus*, de trees demselves will make deir leaves significant soon! and you will confess! *que jamais! jamais!* nor for graces, nor for perfections, deir exists not so charming a place in de world as Troitska! *Et pourquoi, mon enfant? I did make it myself*, I work'd with de masons at de walls, I put in de little trees in deir holes, 'twas mine own hands done dat. I draw de plans, and towsend of my peasant help'd with their hatchet. I was not rich den, as I am now, and so I did make de oeconomist *en tout plein* des choses.'

Sunday, 23rd March [1806]
I don't know what I was going to tell you the day before yesterday when the Princess came wandering into my room from Matty's, with a large orange rind in her hand, and a most beautiful pearl necklace (compos'd of four strings of very fine oriental ones) cramm'd into it, which she bid me tell her, the apothecary had sent her for her throat.

The conceit of this rejoic'd her to such a pitch, that she never ceased glorying, and striding about the room, and abusing every physician upon the face of the Earth and laughing (or rather crowing) at her having satiriz'd them by this means, of sending pearls instead of pills!

I want to know whether these trifles give you an idea of her? She is the greatest oddity upon earth, tho' the causes of my saying so, are not comprised in the circumstances I relate. . . .

150

I will take you down stairs to the hall, where dozens of slaves are waiting with their offerings of bread and salt to greet the Princess! When she appears, they fall down before her and kiss the ground, with that senseless obeisance, that stupefaction feels at the approach of superior power! Her lenity makes their lot better perhaps than that of others! but that's saying very little for the system. Each noble is omnipotent. He may be either an angel or a devil! The chance is on the latter side, and it must be almost an angel indeed who is not ruin'd by the possession of uncontroul'd authority!

I look upon every noble as an iron link in the massy chain that manacles this realm, and, as to the individuals amongst them that I have met at Moscow, 'tis impossible to be in their company without recollecting that they are subjects under a despotism. For in their judgements *bad and good* literally appears to be synonymous with *favour and disgrace*. The idea attach'd to what arises from *character*, always gives place to *office*, and the exterior of deference can be calculated by the Court Almanack much better than by the chronicle of friendship. . . .

Troitskoe.   Monday 27th June 1806 [to Anna Chetwood]
Just conceive *miles* of the most exquisite lily of the valley. After bathing before breakfast, we drive to the forests, which are a succession of fragrance. There are two kinds of Russian plants (one call'd the 'Belle de Mist') and both in the stile of lily of the valley, only more beautiful! These at present embellish the woods, together with heaths, strawberries, wild pinks and roses. . . .

This last week has been one of infinite dissipation, to us all – the house has been full of company, and amongst them a favourite nephew of the Princess's has been here with his wife and little daughter. To amuse ourselves one evening, we drove to a part of this estate, where the Princess has not been for eight years. She was not of the party, but her nephew proposed we shou'd astonish her with a *fête champêtre*, in one of the most romantic spots I ever saw!

151

As it was all wild and entangled, it became necessary to *humanize* it for the occasion – so that in secret, the village of Yarkonoff (which is the name of the place) was let loose, together with six or seven of her nephew's servants, and in four days, the intire was perfectly concluded!

During these days, we used all in succession, to drive off, at untoward hours, to superintend the work. I lived these literally during the mornings, as I have established a rule never to appear till dinner, and consequently am not suspected.

We made a lovely cascade tumble down a natural cave – brought grotesque stones – sodded the ground – made seats – and at length decoy'd the Princess, who to her amazement found herself seated at a collation of fruits, cream etc. – encircled with villagers, singing and dancing, all in their gala dresses, with garlands tied for the occasion.

I believe I described Troitska to you as dead flat, and so it is, for a considerable circle about the house. But this Yarkonoff, is like a little Switzerland, and extends for four versts, in the same romantic view. 'Tis now the bone of *contention* in the family – we all want it to communicate by a winding walk to Troitska – and to have a temple built there, walks made etc. etc. but the Princess *skulks into her shell*, says she is too old, and protests *Troitska* is an earthly Paradise! Matty has at length battled it out with her, and we have just heard that she has surrendered at discretion. . . .[4]

Sadly they were not long to remain so happy at Troitskoe.

Matty had been three years in Russia. Heightened perhaps by the continuing menace of Napoleon, she longed to return to Ireland to see her family. But as she confided to her journal on 22 July, 'the possibility of my going to Ireland even for one year was to produce anguish [in the Princess] which I knew not how to combate. Yet everlasting separation like this implys is dreadful and must not be.'[5]

The following day Katherine tackled the Princess on Matty's behalf. She was almost certainly afraid that should Matty stay on in Russia and the Princess die suddenly, her sister would be cut off in a foreign country with no means of support.

'Kitty had a long conversation with the Princess before breakfast this morning,' wrote Matty 'Such a conversation! She has enter'd into all her views, and the P. is to write a letter to-day to the Empress Mother recommending me to her protection in case I should have the misfortune to lose my beloved Princess.'[6]

The Princess wrote to the Empress, and in due course received a favourable reply. In addition she laid aside £3,000 with the guardians of the Foundling Hospital funds on which Matty could draw in case of need. With matters thus satisfactorily settled they packed up for Moscow.

They arrived in the first week of August to be confronted by another crisis. An English friend reported that Madame Scherbenin, the Princess's alienated daughter, had been spreading slander about the two sisters.

The Princess's daughter was certainly jealous of her mother's affection for Matty, of the large sums of money, the valuable presents showered upon her, of the patronage Matty was said to exercise in the name of the Princess.

Matty had indeed laughingly described herself as the 'Prime Minister' of the Princess, and how 'in the beginning of my Ministry before I understood these State affairs I was often offer'd bribes . . . in the guise of proferr'd friendship, Music, lace, boxes, even sweetmeats and Wine . . .'[7]

But Madame Scherbenin had also accused her of influencing the Princess to persuade her son to divorce his wife and marry Matty; of later causing strife between the Prince and his mother; of being a sorceress and casting spells, of being a danger to the state. Certainly Matty now found herself in a seemingly insoluble dilemma, 'not knowing how to stay here or how to quit my beloved Princess whose happiness appears to be link'd with my stay.'[8]

For a time, it seems, the two sisters were able to conceal these reports from the Princess (who, in fact, already knew of them) for half way through the month they all set off for a nine day pilgrimage to the Loretto of Russia, the Convent of Troitza, about thirty miles north of Moscow.

A carriage full of cooks, kitchen utensils, a butler and silver side-board preceded them as they wound their way past noblemen's seats to pause *briefly at Madame Nebalsin's for the night. 'Baths! Dairies! Hot Houses! English Oeconomy! Studs of Horses! Dwarfs!'[9] Katherine recorded in manner impressionistic.*

At the Convent they gazed at the shrine of St Sergius whose 'famish'd shrunk black finger' the Princess kissed, then they passed on to Lake Perislaff and the holy town of Rostov.

They were back in Moscow before the end of July, but the Scherbenin affair was still continuing its virulent course.

'The subject of Madame Scherbenin is like a spunge to our existence,' wrote Matty on 28 August. 'We are not capable of doing anything.'[10]

Katherine, however, made an attempt, and wrote to Madame Scherbenin. Unfortunately Madame Scherbenin's reply was by mistake brought not to Katherine, but to Matty, who was with the Princess, and in a moment everything came to light, 'and we have had a dreadful explanation with the Princess. "tis shocking,' added Matty, 'to think 'tis from her daughter all this misery arises.'[11]

'What a day we have had!' she wrote the following day. 'Letters Conversations, Hysterics, terrors. Good heaven what a day of Misery!'[12]

Thankfully, by early Autumn they were back at Troitskoe again, more than content to occupy themselves with making a transcript of the Princess's Memoirs. In this occupation Katherine made the English translation from the Princess's French, which Matty in turn copied out. From time to time the Princess leaned over their shoulders affectionately and made corrections, borrowing the girls' pens. . . .

Troitskoe.   21st October 1806 [to her sister Harriet]
I believe since the ages of Tom Thumb there never were such doleful attempts at composition as amongst the Russians! These twelve months, I have been dying for the books of the country, and at length they gave me one so celebrated that it had been translated into *all languages*. But I protest, the most deplorably affected novel that ever dissolved the heart of a mantua maker was *Shakespear* in comparison of what I found it! So what can one do?

As to the conversations amongst the young bears,* 'tis

* Russians.

154

nothing but about their pairs and tails, and as to the married gentry, 'tis uniformly about their family affairs and expences.

You must know that every woman has the right over her own fortune totally independent of her husband, and he is as independent of his wife. Marriage therefore is no union of interests whatsoever, and the wife, if she has a large estate, and happens to marry a poor man, is still consider'd rich, while the husband may go to jail without one farthing of her possessions being responsible for him! This gives a curious sort of hue to the conversations of the Russian matrons, which to a meek English woman, appears prodigious independence in the midst of a despotic government!

At first I thought the men bewitch'd when in the circle before dinner, a snuff box, or toothpick case has been exhibited as the gift of their wives, on such a *jour de fête*, or *jour de nom*. And the wives in like manner, gravely boasting, of having receiv'd a present from their husbands of a Turkish shawl or embroider'd reticule or earring or bracelet. But I was still more surprised when inquiries were made for a lady not yet return'd to Moscow, and her husband replied, that she was making some inquiries on her estate in the Ukraine, and that she had some idea of selling it, from the extreme inconvenience of the distance which seperated it from his! So that when a party of ladies talk together in a group, one is sure of affairs! affairs! affairs! being the subject, except when a coquettish one, attracts the general attention by the exhibition of a diamond wreath or necklace, which she immediately tells you, cost *so many hundred slaves*, for in making considerable purchases, the land goes without mercy, and the *slaves* remain like the trees, which pass from one possessor to another.

And this brings me to one general observation, which is that the landed property of this Imperial Realm is (from unconscientious extravagance of the nobles) passing like wild-fire to the merchants, who are in Russia, neither more nor less than pedlars and shopkeepers, and (exactly as they did in France before the Revolution) the princes of the country are breaking down all ideal barriers, and marrying the daughters of the merchants as fast as they can! This, however, may not lead exactly to the same catastrophe, for *here* there is no pride of birth to be wounded, and 'tis comical enough to reflect, that Peter the Great (who was the most iron despot that ever scourged the earth) has form'd, under the name of an aristocratic despotism, the most absolute disregard to birth, and in this respect the most compleat Republic I believe that the world contains.

The clue to this labyrinth of paradox is the military power being the sole standard of honor! So that if the son of a shoe maker (and a free man) was made a captain, he would take precedence of the first nobleman in Russia who happen'd to be only a lieutenant.

Therefore the high spirit of aristocracy, with all the beauty of ancestry, (which has cut the throat of so many nations, and made such lovely romances and poems) no more exists within a single Russian mind, that I have ever met with, than sun beams within cucumbers,* or any other monstrous incongruity. . . .

This letter has been lying several days in my desk, and I never recollected it. God knows what I intended saying to you, but since I have compleatly snapt the thread of my discourse, I will pop upon the very first idea that comes into my head, and that is a Georgian Prince, whom I saw at Moscow last August . . . at a grand entertainment given at the Emperor's expence in the Kremlin. . . .

These tributary Princes to Russia were only just arrived as sort of prisoners to the Emperor! Their country has long been under the Imperial yoke, but not liking the controul they suffer'd, the principal one, (a haughty turbulent daring looking mustach'd savage) united himself with the Persians and was caught in arms fighting against the Russian power. His son (a fine young man of seventeen) was with him, and had the most melancholy expression of countenance, while on the contrary his father

---

* Relating to the foolish experiments made at the Academy of Lagado in Swift's *Gulliver's Travels*.

seem'd diverted at the novelty of European scenes, and never ceased making enquiries from his interpreter of everything that pass'd, at the same time shewing by his demeanour, the most haughty consciousness of superiority.

I was amused at contemplating this fallen King, with all his Asiatic retinue, as they sat opposite to me at a brilliant banquet, which terminated the entertainment, as I caught a glimpse of their mustachios, and bare throats, scarfs, and diamond rings, through the spreading branches of fruit trees, which shaded all the table with the most refreshing green. . . .

If nothing interferes, I think about April we shall set out for the confines of Poland, visit the Princess's estate at Krougla, and so thro' Courland, make the best of our way to Riga, by which I shall escape all the horrors of the Finland Gulph.

And now, since I have room to spare, I believe I will fill up the chinks with another story, which is more curious than you will be inclined to think, because it is one of the most national vestiges of antiquity existing,* which with the peculiar costume of the people! their musical instruments! village amusements! auguries! and superstition, prove that (from the strong similitude with the Greeks in these matters) both have drawn their origin from the self same nation . . . the *Vapour Bath*, (that universal panacea in this country) remains to illustrate itself, in the present instance of Sophia's marriage (Matty's *femme de chambre*) which took place here the other day with infinite *éclat*.

The solemnities of the day before marriage, consist in being bless'd by the images and going to the Bath. Tho' I had attended several weddings in church I never had the courage to suffocate myself in the cause of seeing things with my own eyes. However, I was resolved not to quit the country without doing so, and therefore here goes for the operation from beginning to end!

The Bride elect, *dissolved in tears*, sat at the top of a table

---

* Katherine Wilmot and her sister were among the first travellers to recognize the importance of the Russian peasant culture. See Journal of *Slavonic and East European Studies* Vol. 66, No. 1, 1988.

(previous to the bathing business) which was laid out with emblematic fruits. Presently, the bridegroom presented her with her toilette and then disappear'd and was conducted to *his* bath by his companions! This toilette consisted of every necessary article together with rouge and white paint. A group of girls then set up what sounded a sort of requiem call'd *Pesi Swadbischnia!**

As I was curious to root into the marrow of the business, I was resolved to comprehend the meaning of what was sung, which has been sung time out of mind, and many of these allegoric compositions still remain in the Slavonian dialect, the change of name only being necessary to make it perfectly appropriate.

Here then is a specimen of one amongst fifty of the same nature, which was sung at the pitch of their voices.

On the top of a high mountain, dark with forests were seen a flock of Wild Geese and a group of Swans. A young Cygnet stray'd in amongst the geese who all began to peck at her and drive her off! On which the Cygnet cried out,

'Oh! do not treat me so in pity! for 'tis much against my inclination that I find myself where I am, and nothing but the Tempest could have forced me in amongst you!'

Alas! this is the picture of our dear Sophia whom we are about to lose, who, finding herself entangled in a troop of hymeneals, weeps with bitterness, and like the young Cygnet cries,

'Do not treat me harshly good people, 'tis not from my own impulse I am come amongst you, but the Kabitka and the horses of Timothy have driven me hither!'

We then attended her to the Bath with all her young companions, amounting to between thirty and forty girls, who assisted in undressing her in the outer chamber, and then led her (in a flood of tears) naked into the Bath. They then took off their own cloaths, and after scouring her to their hearts' content,

* Wedding songs.

danced round about (in all their national dances) clapping their hands, and drinking wine, which was dispensed by another Eve, who sat with a bottle in one hand, and a glass in the other, her long tresses falling down about her shoulders which, like all the others was the only shadow of covering they could boast. They then set up a universal song, of which this that follows is the translation.

A wild Pigeon dipping itself in the sea, after having flutter'd its beautiful pinions, cried,

'How can I quit the waters? How soar above the high and rugged mountains? But the cold of winter comes! Its frosts will penetrate! The snow will cover the entire ground! In spite of myself I *must* quit the waters. In spite of myself I *must* quit the dangers of these rugged shores!'

In this manner and with these reflections our dear companion Sophia bathes, and paints her face with red and white, and blackens her eyebrows like jet! After which she bursts into tears and exclaims,

'How can I quit my Father? How abandon my Mother? 'Tis in spite of myself I quit my Father! 'Tis in spite of myself I bid adieu to my Mother!'

I believe we stay'd above an hour at the Bath which became the most festive scene imaginable. They colour'd themselves for sport in the most ridiculous manner and sang and danced like a troop of Bachanals, while the bride continued mute, and in a flood of tears. At length she was conducted back to the house and again took her seat at the table, while all her companions sang the following song.

Here then begins the marriage of our dear Sophia. All the young girls stand with her about the table, and even take honourable places, but she is herself above them all, tho' 'tis she who makes the humblest bow to her companions, whilst she ruminates seriously on thoughts which do not torment their festive hearts!

159

'How' (she thinks) 'can I bear to reflect on the idea of a severe Father-in-Law! How can I bear to think on the idea of a severe Mother-in-Law! I must call her (in spite of myself) Mother. She would be offended if I did not! Oh! how I must trample on my pride to call my Father-in-Law Father, and my Mother-in-Law, Mother!'

After several trifling ceremonies the whole affair ended in a very handsome supper, and the next day the couple were married. . . .

15 November 1806 – 17 September 1807

By 15 November they were back in Moscow again though Katherine, who had begun making preparations for her return to England, mutinously recorded she would much rather have spent winter in the peace of Troitskoe.

Moscow had become associated for both sisters with 'Perplexity distress and sorrow'.[1] Furthermore, as Katherine expressed it in a letter home, she had now seen for herself 'the total apathy there exists on the sentiment of honor, in the daily practices of the high born, and great, and powerful. . . . God knows whether this is a national characteristic or not, I believe the best, because the Russian peasantry are the best hearted beings upon earth, the most innocent and guiltless. But the gentlemen are those I speak of. . . .'[2]

But graver issues were already occupying their attention, soon causing every moment 'to team with alarm'. At the end of October news had come through of a French victory at Jena over Prussia, Russia's ally. Early in November Napoleon began moving his army towards Poland. At the end of the month he was approaching Warsaw.

The Russian Emperor's Governor immediately ordered all French out of the Empire, almost an impossibility, as Matty explained, since the country swarmed with French milliners, dancing masters, waiting maids, cooks, booksellers, physicians, not to mention tutors and governesses.

'These have prepared their pupils' minds for the silken yoke of the Tyrant,' wrote Matty, 'whom the Lord send may be caught at last by the excess of his ambition, and frozen into the land he is now resolv'd to conquer – I mean Russia. . . . Public events here wear so menacing an aspect that Heaven only knows what may happen between this and K.'s departure.'[3]

The English merchants were already donating arms to help the

161

Emperor, Katherine reported, the Russian merchants at St Petersburg contributing two million, those at Moscow, one million roubles, while the nobles were raising a militia to guard the country.

'We are struck with terror at the idea of this militia! The Russian slaves (which of course compose it) having under Paul made many desperate efforts for their liberty, and now what may they not do – when they have arms in their hands? and when the troops march to the frontiers against the French?

'The French have seiz'd Mundin, Paderborn, Magdabourg, Castrin, Stettin and Warsaw,'⁴ she listed sombrely.

The new year of 1807 opened in gathering confusion, 'a web of political intrigue,' according to Katherine, with rumours of a possible revolution in favour of the Empress Mother, a purported victory over the French – '6,000 cut to pieces' – though not verified. On 9 January, as the Princess was entertaining, news came, totally unexpected, that her son, Prince Dashkov, was at death's door.

The Wilmots were thrown into a desperate state of anxiety knowing this would jeopardize their renewed hope that the Princess might allow Matty to go back to Ireland with her sister. On the 17th news of the Prince's death confirmed their fears.

Katherine, overcome as much on her sister's as on the Princess's account, was instantly prostrated with 'a rheumatic nervous headache', which for some time prohibited even writing.

The Prince's death and subsequent funeral, which the Princess appears not to have attended, led to further and more violent confrontation between her English guests and her daughter.

'Madame Scherbenin as chief mourner stood close by the coffin,' wrote Matty, 'but stood as the Daemon of Revenge, not as the agoniz'd sister of a brother who was but too kind to her.

'Her eyes wander'd round the church and whispers between her and her companions soon shew'd me that I was the object of her enquiry. With me she saw Anna Petrovna. All intercourse between them had been at an end for many months, but rushing by seven or six ladys who separated, in a loud and peircing tone of voice she told her that she too had lost a friend, and that her brother had spoken of her the 8th day of his illness ('tis certain he was at that time insensible) *and*

162

without stopping she added, "don't let those English monsters *approach him."*

'*As she spoke in Russ and I paid no attention, I did not know the purport of her words but imagin'd she was in hysterics 'till A.P. explain'd them; nor could I for a moment comprehend the possibility of a human creature much less a sister being occupied in such a way at such a moment; but so it was, and that evidently to insult her Mother, for to the present moment she has never seen my face tho' I saw hers, for I was cover'd with a thick black veil. . . .'[5]*

Both sisters recognized Matty's worsening dilemma. As she herself said, honour urged her to stay with the Princess, while anxiety for her own safety urged departure.

'*Kitty suffers a million times more than I do,' she wrote, 'for I don't know what sort of insensibility (or perhaps 'tis a support from heaven) makes me fearless in spight of reason, and in the midst of communications which tend to show how perfectly devoid of faith, honour, honesty or anything but vicious propensity and actions, are the great bulk of this Empire.'[6]*

Keenly aware that she was in actual danger from her enemies, she informed her family she was sending over £5,000 when the exchange rate rose, adding, '*by the by I shall not die a day the sooner for lightening my mind by saying here that in case of my death I wish my property to be equally divided amongst my brothers and sisters to whatever amount it may be. . . .'[7]*

Yet for all her courage she dreaded Katherine's departure.

'*I wish to God she was not so necessary to the happiness and existence of the Princess as she is. . . .'[8]* Katherine confided in a letter which also explained how for safety, since the contents were politically highly dangerous, she intended hiding the completed manuscript of the *Princess's* Memoirs '*about my own person'** when she returned to England.

The common sense of danger throughout the country was by now giving rise to numerous reports of ominous signs and portents. Both Wilmots recorded one which 'everyone believes' of a guard hearing

---

* This was the only copy that reached England as Matty was forced to destroy hers.

163

the sound of horses prancing behind the closed doors of the great Cathedral of the Kremlin. On going to unlock the doors to discover the cause of the disturbance, they flew open of their own accord to reveal, in a blaze of candles, two armed warriors bowing before the Virgin of Kazan, patron of the Cathedral. The warriors withdrew, mounted their waiting chargers, who were impatiently 'fluttering a thousand wings', and flew heavenwards, crying out they were going to the aid of their countrymen against the French.

Four days after, the French and Russian armies engaged at Eylau in a blinding snowstorm. But the battle was tragically inconclusive, and almost half the combatants lost their lives.

It was now that a more domestic angel arrived at the Princess's in the shape of her daughter-in-law, the recently widowed young Princess Dashkov. Disapproving of her son's marriage, the old Princess had for twenty years refused to meet her, but had now summoned her.

'Interesting, able and very charming,'[9] was Katherine's immediate verdict, while of the meeting between the two Princesses Matty wrote, 'Tears on both sides, and scarcely a word fill'd up the five minutes which it lasted . . .'[10]

'Thank Heaven I can speak of them now as of a mother and daughter seemingly born to fulfil the happiness of each other,'[11] wrote Katherine, who no doubt hoped the newcomer might absorb some of the excessive affection being poured out on Matty.

Certainly, from now on, a more tranquil mood settled on the Princess's household. Tired as she was, Katherine was nevertheless soon describing 'Cossacks, Bashkirs, Calmouks and Kirgis' passing through Moscow late in February to attack the French on the borders of Poland. 'The most extraordinary undisciplined swarm I ever beheld,' she wrote of the Bashkirs, 'we saw about 1,040 ride thro' Moscow, their horses not larger than asses, and all shaggy and filthy, the men were not far removed from savages . . . and they had the appearance of being rak'd together from 4 fag ends of creation. They eat their horses, and have no objection to human flesh, when they can get it. . . .'[12]

She was impressed by the Cossacks, however, who at the Princess's request especially put on an extempore display of martial gymnastics.

Two days later the Princess, Anna Petrovna and the Wilmots set out *on a four-day pilgrimage to the Monastery of New Jerusalem to attend a service for the soul of Prince Dashkov, the Princess afterwards donating five hundred roubles for a chapel to commemorate the family.*

'They are in the most deplorable distress for some swinging relic to attract pilgrims* and then the donations would recompense all with tributory gold!'[13] Katherine dryly commented.

Although she herself was still experiencing 'universal derangement' and weakness caused by the anxieties of the last miserable weeks, the new-found calm reigning in the Princess's household continued. This even when the servants arrived in a body to report a conspiracy set afoot by Madame Scherbenin, 'to bewitch and destroy the Princess, the young Princess, and Matty'.[14] An event that 'has blown over miraculously,' commented Katherine, and went on to record rejoicings for the Princess's sixty-third birthday.

The Princess meanwhile employed herself rearranging her cabinet of natural history exhibits which she intended presenting to the university of Moscow; made various legacies in anticipation of her imminent death; extirpated her daughter from her will, and began preparing for Easter.

'Thank God Easter week is over,' Katherine wrote on 3 May, 'the bells are silent for the 1st time for 8 days and 8 nights. . . .'[15] 'What have we done this week?' she asked herself a few days later. 'I have no answer to the question, or rather I can only reply like a cabbage, I have vegetated!'[16] There was nonetheless cause for quiet satisfaction: letters from home after a long silence, the pleasing fact that the Princess had for seventeen thousand roubles bought a new house for her daughter-in-law.

The young Princess had recently been spending almost every evening with the Princess and her household, and Matty expressed herself more pleased with her every day. Yet although the old Princess had been given another daughter, she still could not find it in her heart, it seems, to part with Matty.

---

* A situation familiar to readers of Dostoievsky's *The Brothers Karamazov*. The Empress Catherine II had confiscated the once-extensive lands of the church, reducing many monasteries to poverty.

165

Moscow.   June 16th 1807 [to Anna Chetwood]
My departure is the present motive of our operations. Every
evening we make excursions to the exquisite environs of
Moscow in open carriages, and wander amongst the beautiful
improvements of Neskushna, Astanka, Tzaritzen* etc. etc. etc.
Oh! indeed these places are lovely beyond measure! The
convents and monasterys too, (which are encircled with walls
and turrets like ancient fortifications) are objects of our examination, and the celebrated one of Donskoy, which domineers over
the Asiatic Moscow, was the last where we paid our devotions
and drank lemonade like so many smoking Turks, under the
shade of weeping birch, which veils the entire country, and
through the green branches of which all the yellow domes, and
gilded towers and crosses blaze from amidst the Kremlin with
the most magnificent splendour. . . .

*It was proving difficult for even Katherine to leave the hospitable
Princess. 'I have been anxious for some weeks on the subject of my
departure,' she wrote in her private journal on 14 June. 'The Princess
had for months past made plans to accompany me to Riga, but her own ill
health and various other matters have created obstacles – however, she
wants me to accompany her to Troitskoe, and should she not be able to
fulfill her intentions now, then in August. But that would be too late for
me, and I have finally persuaded her to let me leave without her. These
last weeks have been taken up with preparations – the painter has made
alterations to my sister's portrait, and he has done one of A.P. for me,
and one of me for her.'†[17]*

*The day she wrote was a fateful one – the anniversary of the battle of
Marengo, the day Napoleon inflicted total defeat on the Russian army at
Friedland. The news, however, took some time to reach them, for on the
28th of the month Katherine noted that, 'all the bells of Moscow have*

---

* Famous country estates.

† Both Wilmots had their portraits painted in Russia. Katherine's was considered a
particularly good likeness. '. . . I never saw so flattering a picture, so like, tho' 'tis
less so, from my growing every day thinner'. (Transcript *Katherine Wilmot's letters from
Russia*) p. 149; Royal Irish Academy).

been ringing for a victory gained over the French by the Russians in the neighbourhood of Konigsberg', adding, 'which I am afraid is not confirmed perfectly'.[18]

A few days later she described everyone as agonized on the subject of public news from the armies. In the end it was as she had feared, 'Konigsberg they report is taken by the French. But lies is the only intellectual food of Moscow and with this food we have been gorged almost to death.'[19]

It was time to leave. Last visits were made to their Moscow friends, then on 4 July, the Princess, the young Princess, Anna Petrovna and Matty set out from Moscow to accompany Katherine part of the way to St Petersburg, the first leg of her journey home.

The night was spent at the Monastery of the New Jerusalem, which they had visited in March, and where their friend, the Archimandrate, greeted them in his 'lilac gown and black monkish hood'. The following day they drove to Klin. Here, next morning, Katherine finally left them.

'Tuesday morning previous to the moment of my setting off was wheez'd *away in the usual anticipation of sorrow preceding a last and dying Adieu!' she wrote in her private journal. 'I settled this last point however with the Princess, and* run *away without bidding mortal adieu.*

'Ellen [Cavanagh] had been taken ill which alarmed us, however she was tolerably recovered, and about eleven I drove off so heartily reliev'd from the weight of spirits I had so long endured from the last year on Matty's account from its being irrevocably fix'd that she sh'd return next year. . . .'[20]

Petersburg.   July 15th [1807] [to Anna Chetwood]
Ivan Alexandrovitch, the trusty Police Officer, follow'd in his Kibitka, with my provisions for the way, and of course I had nothing to do but to fan myself as he battled for the horses, paid the postillions, order'd eggs and hot water for my tea, (the only articles with which the cottages furnish travellers excepting milk which is the best in the world).

* To Ireland.

Sunday morning we stop'd within a few miles of Petersburgh at the palace of Tzarsko Selo, (belonging to the Emperor and built by Catherine II) which I examined and so arrived here Sunday the 11th July at the house of the Baron d'Hoggier, who was Dutch Ambassador here during the time of Catherine II.

Baroness Hoggier is *own* niece to Princess Daschkaw, and an old acquaintance of mine. Her husband I knew but little of before, but I am excessively pleased with his benevolent roughness, and worth. He is a great castle of a man, with large features and agreeable countenance, possessing a great deal of sense.

This is the fourth day I have been here. . . . I am to go down in a barge from this door, (as the house is situated on the Neva) on Friday the 23rd of this month, to Cronstadt where, I shall step into my old berth on board of Captain Clark's ship *The Good Intent*, the same which brought Matty, and the same in which I came to Russia. . . .

Yesterday the Peace between the Emperor and Bonaparte was announced.* This house is just opposite the fortress from whence the cannon roar'd all day, and illuminations blazed all night through the town. Heaven knows whether these are to be taken as demonstrations of real joy. . . .

Everyone rails against the English, for being such dilatory allies. The ignoramuses (who are ninety-nine to one) snarl against England, the others attribute it to the opposition principles, which were at the helm, but all the Bears to a cub grumble against us. . . .

Passport difficulties kept Katherine chafing at St Petersburg until the end of July.

'I am sick of journalizing,' she wrote on the 25th, 'as I write to Matty, and the Princess and A.Petrovna every hands turn. This is the reason I can't particularize. All this week I've been led the life of a dog about my passport. I have forfeited my sailing with Captain Clark and now all my

---

* The Treaty of Tilsit, an aggressive pact for the ruin of England.

papers are in the College of Commerce, and must be signed by Count Romanzow (who is the chief) before I get my passport from the Governor.'[21]

As it turned out she was not to get a ship until the 1st of August, and this only because the excellent Mr Cavanagh secured her a berth, flew off to get her passport signed at the Custom House, and hurried her on board just as the ship was getting under weigh.

Safely on board she relaxed to record her feelings of satisfaction, 'So on board the Elbe, *I am sole mistress not only of my little state cabin, but of the large one, as the only additional passenger is another captain of a vessel, Captain Salter. Everything is as clean as a pin. I have a chest of drawers to lay my cloaths in and every possible conveniency. This is a three masted vessel, laden with isinglass, iron, tea, deal, beeswax, linen and tallow. There are a few* Quakers *(as they call wooden cannons), the stay sails (or steering sails) are filling with the east wind which promises us a good voyage.'[22]*

However, she was soon writing: 'Tuesday, Wednesday Thursday, we have not advanced very far and when I say I have walked the deck, wrote, laugh'd at the cook, Edward the Black Prince, *help'd to make the pudding, read and slept, I have nothing more to record in my* log *book. I did not get up all day there was so much movement in the ship. Friday the wind contrary, and Saturday a storm preceded by lightning. Sunday the wind favourable, and we're* out *of the Finland Gulf.'[23]*

Bad weather was to come: 'desperate squalls which brought great confusion in the cabbin. The sea came in at the window opposite my bed and wet all my sheets. My writing case was soak'd through, and all my bag of books and ink. From the rocking of the vessel all the table full of decanters, glasses and dishes were whisk'd all about incessantly, tho' I did my best to defend myself against it by holding the posts. . . .'[24]

The 'eternal creaking' of the ship prevented her from sleeping, and whenever the weather allowed she lay out on deck. Meanwhile, Captain Salter regaled her with tales of his escapes from the French, 'of water spouts in the Adriatic, of balls of fire breaking over his vessel, of escaping wrecks, of battling with the Navy men who press'd *his men etc. etc. etc.'.[25]*

On board the Elbe, *Captain Landells.   Saturday 15th August [1807]*
[to her sister Alicia]

I will pass over the monotony of my voyage hitherto and bring you to the deck yesterday morning at eight o'clock when we sail'd up right before the town of Copenhagen.

A pilot came on board immediately from shore and speaking very bad English he puzzled out that England and Denmark* had declared war, and, pointing to the three crown batteries and floating batteries, which were all ready primed to fire upon us! he added that four hundred English transports full of troops, and several men of war were lying off Elsineur twenty miles off and that the Danish guard ship there, had slipped her cables and sail'd away to Norway. A strict prohibition had been given to prevent the pilots going to the British vessels, to guide them through the sound, and that he did not know why, but that prohibition had been taken off that very morning, which made him conclude that the countrys had come to an accommodation.

Some time afterwards, a gun boat laden with supplies, for Stralsund, spoke to us, and caution'd Captain Landells to keep to the Swedish side, as we sail'd to Elsineur. As you may conclude we look'd rather foolish at each other, for had an action commenced we have not a single gun to defend us! I cannot *affect* to say I was frightened *for I was too near the danger* and therefore I set about making up my mind for whatever might come to pass.

We had a deplorably slow wind, so that we did not anchor before the town of Elsineur, till seven in the evening. I prepared all my letters for Russia and my draft upon the Danish banker for the captain to take on shore, when an order arrived to say, 'None of the English must attempt to land!' The captain sail'd off to one of the English ships and did not return till ten o'clock. In the meantime I knew Matty would have died of distress if she had not receiv'd a letter from Elsineur, and yet no possible means were there to send one. Just by the dint of good luck, a little boat

* At the Treaty of Tilsit, Denmark was to be forced to join Russia and France and their fleet taken over. In this engagement Copenhagen was besieged and the Danish fleet secured for England.

170

boarded us, and through the means of the person on board I had one sent to the Swedish post, which eased my mind.

We were surrounded by four hundred transports, twelve men of war, and one hundred traders, all English. The bugle horn sounded most delightfully, the military music play'd, and really nothing could be more thoroughly warlike! Just then the definitive answer arrived from the Crown Prince of Denmark, 'that Zealand should not be ceded, that he would defend it to the last drop of his blood, and he would bury himself amongst the ruins of old Croninsburg Castle, rather than consent to the demands of the English!' Nothing therefore remain'd but for Admiral Gambier* to give orders to fire upon the town and castle. But the wind did not serve to land the troops and therefore the night escaped without a battle!

In the meantime we received orders from Commodore Moth (who commands the *Prince William*, our convoy) to prepare for sailing instantly for England this morning, which we duly obey'd, and here we are, already out of sight of Elsineur, and *all the fun*, as the sailors call it.

Had it been possible *bravely* to have got into a safe nook or corner, I own I should like to have witness'd the affair, which will be tremendous. And from the circumstances of the Danes (Heaven pity them, they have been used basely) one cannot doubt of the success of the British.

You will say that the Fates have *soaped my tail* for me, I have so often slip't through the fingers of the enemy! And really 'tis amazing my luck *now* in not being *one* day later, for in that case we should inevitably have been obliged to have sail'd back to Russia. As while the sound was on fire (which it will be tomorrow) the English would not have had time to think of protecting us, while they were vanquishing a Kingdom! . . .

The Elbe *was now slipping warily past Kronberg Castle, 'with three*

---

* James Gambier (1756–1833), 1st Lord Gambier, later commander of the Channel fleet.

tiers of cannon pointed'. A passing ship signalled that a Russian man-of-war had fired on them from Riga, 'from the report of England and Russia having declared war'.[26]

Monday [17th August]	*We were fishing all day.*
Tuesday [18th]	*We caught plenty of mackrill for our dinner. A man-of-war sail'd close with a band of music playing.*
Wednesday [19th]	*We caught a* **Devil Fish** *that groans and growls. I heard it several times after 'twas caught on deck. . . .*
Thursday [20th]	*Oh Heavens we shall never be out of this cursed categut. We have all last night drifted towards the Swedish coast . . . in short this is the 5th day and I believe we have not advanced a 100 miles from Elsineur and I am tired to death of my voyage for want of companions and books, having exhausted all mine. . . .*
Friday [21st]	*While I walk on deck at night I hear the bird called the killick cry about the ship. Captain S[alter] says it lays its eggs while in the water, and hatches them under its wings,* **diving** *(with the young beneath its wings) till they are old enough to take care of themselves.*
Saturday [22nd]	*We make no sort of progress! . . . the purchase of this ship is 5,000 guineas, each saylor (there are 12) is paid by the Captain 5 guineas a month and the cook 6. The cable and anchor cost £200 – the wages of the Mate is £7 a month.*[27]

By the beginning of the next week Katherine had run out of anything to record, and even Captain Salter seems to have run out of tall stories.

'This entire week has been misery and sufferings past endurance which we have past in the catigat and Skaw,* and we have been reduced

---

* The northernmost point of Denmark.

172

to death's door, and I am sure I have suffer'd to the extent of my powers of endurance.'[28]

On 31 August the wind grew favourable, but the remainder of the week was miserable, 'with such squalls and hurricanes as was terrific. We split all our sails and were for putting into the Humber.'[29]

On 7 September they at last touched in at Yarmouth.

'Oh my God such Heaven as a little repose, cleanliness and fresh provisions is after such wicked privation in all these things as we have sustained these 5 long weeks!' Katherine wrote. 'I thought we should have worship'd the first loaf of bread we had and then the basket of apples and plumbs! In short all our woes were forgotten in the luxury of the common necessarys of life.'[30]

The voyage was almost done, though for Tuesday and Wednesday they 'toss'd about at anchor' until Thursday, when a fair wind took them to Gravesend. Here they disembarked and put up at the Falcon Inn. On Saturday one of Katherine's Wilmot relations called for them in a chaise and drove them up to London to the comfort of Osborne's Family Hotel.

Postscript

It was not until 16 October that Matty heard of Katherine's safe arrival in England, by which time her sister had completed a round of visits and was preparing to return to Cork.

'I feel precisely as if those Russian years had been a dream,'[1] she wrote, staying comfortably with cousins at Bruce Castle. Although longing to see her family she dreaded returning to the cold and damp of Ireland, recalling with pleasure the comfortable Russian stoves, how even outside, the Russian air had been crisp and dry, 'with the effect of champagne or high bottled cyder'. In Russia she had hardly had a cold, and her 'asthma' nothing like so persistent, though no one had then recognized it as the early stages of tuberculosis.

Matty doggedly remained with the Princess for another year. This against the dark background of worsening relations between England and Russia, and the growing unpopularity of the English colony, whose members began gradually to leave the country.

Back at Troitskoe she gamely decided to spend the winter learning Italian, having dancing lessons, lessons on the harp couchée to take her mind off that *'suspension* of friendship' between Russia and England which made her feel 'compleatly in a Labyrinth'.[2]

Unable to bear the Princess's grief at the mere mention of her returning home, Matty seems to have lapsed into a total paralysis of will. Yet the opportunity to leave Russia at all was becoming increasingly curtailed, and early in February 1808 she had the chance to make the return journey to England with friends. She set out in floods of tears, reached St Petersburg where her heart failed her, and returned to the Princess once more.

It was only at the last possible moment that she eventually forced herself to leave, but by then she knew 'the Princess is so grieved and so different from what I apprehended that I cannot support her suffering. I wish I was gone.'[3]

She sailed for England on 26 October 1808, but not before the usual panic and confusion over her passport, and the now customary and angelic intervention of Mr Cavanagh. Worse perhaps, her baggage was ransacked by the Russian Customs who rightly suspected that she was carrying the Princess's *Memoirs*, but wrongly that her collection of musical manuscripts were actually coded messages. Fearful that her friend might be incriminated should the authorities discover the *Memoirs* Matty reluctantly destroyed them.

The voyage, in which she endured shipwreck, and an eight-day sojourn on a remote Swedish island (which, admiring the simple life, she rather enjoyed), at last ended the day after Christmas, when she landed at Harwich.

'How all is changed at Troitskoe,' the Princess was soon mournfully writing, 'the theatre is closed; I have not had a single performance; the pianoforte continues silent; the *femmes de chambre* have ceased to sing. Everything paints your absence and my sorrow.'[4]

She was not long to survive her favourite's departure. On 4 January 1810 she died, forgotten, in her huge Moscow mansion. As she had instructed, her body was taken to Troitskoe and buried there with the simplest ceremony in presence of only a priest and a few of her serfs.

Thereafter, her prized possessions fell away. The great Moscow house and two of her estates had been left to a nephew, who soon sold them off. The Moscow home became a music academy. Troitskoe, which she had loved so much, was looted and destroyed when the French invaded Russia two and a half years after her death. The trees were cut down, the garden statues, the Chinese temple where Matty had read *The Castle of Otranto* in Italian among a field of roses, were carted away for building material, the furniture and the Princess's famous library used for fuel in the villagers' stoves.

Matty herself married a clergyman, and named her first child, Catherine Anne Dashkov, after the Princess. She also kept faith with the Princess, and after a tactful lapse of time, published in 1840 her friend's *Memoirs** translated into English. Something that would have pleased the Princess, who had always been an Anglophil. She died in 1873, two years short of a hundred.

Katherine, as she had feared, eventually found the Irish climate unendurable, and settled in France in the hope of curing her worsening lung condition. She lived first at Moulins and latterly at Paris where, on 28 March 1824, she died at the early age of fifty-one.

Matty, who had always loved and admired her, mourned the 'bright sallies of fancy and force of expression' which had given such zest to her sister's conversation, but nevertheless in her Requiem sought to justify such cleverness in a woman.

She had not 'the cant of religion', she wrote, 'nor perhaps had she its comforts as much as would sooth her friends to reflect upon, but her efforts were sincere, and God sees in secret which the world does not . . .'[5]

---

* Brought back by Katherine.

176

Sources

Manuscript Sources

In all there are five known transcripts of the original manuscript of Katherine Wilmot's Grand Tour with her friend, Lady Mount Cashell. The one used here is in the possession of Colonel A. L. King-Harman OBE DL. It is mentioned in the editorial note to the 1920 published edition of the Tour, and is in all respects the same.

Katherine's Russian Tour is taken from transcripts in the Wilmot MS in the Royal Irish Academy, which also houses the only holograph copy of Katherine's personal journal, this is for the period 26 October 1806 – 23 October 1807.

Books

An Irish Peer on the Continent (1801–1803). Being a narrative of the Tour of Stephen, 2nd. Earl Mount Cashell, through France, Italy, etc., as related by Catherine* *Wilmot*, edited by Thomas U. Sadleir, MA, London, Williams and Norgate, 1920.
The Russian Journals and Letters of Martha and Catherine Wilmot, edited by Lady Londonderry and H. M. Hyde, London, Macmillan, 1934.

Abbreviations

KW: Katherine Wilmot
King-Harman: Transcript owned by Colonel A. L. King-Harman,
               Ouse Manor, Sharnbrook, Beds.
Londonderry: *The Russian Journals and Letters of Martha and Catherine*

---

* Katherine's own spelling of her name is with a 'K'.

Wilmot, edited by Lady Londonderry and H. M. Hyde, London, Macmillan, 1934.

RIA: Royal Irish Academy.

Sadleir: *An Irish Peer on the Continent (1801–1803)*, edited by Thomas U. Sadleir, London, Williams and Norgate, 1920.

Notes

Introduction

1. KW – her sister Alicia, 18 February 1806, Wilmot MS. RIA.
2. *The Journals and Letters of Fanny Burney*, ed Hemlow (1975), p. xxiv.
3. *Sadleir*, p. xiii.
4. KW – her brother Robert, Sunday 13 December 1801, King-Harman.
5. KW – her brother Robert, 3 January 1802, King-Harman.
6. KW – her brother Robert, 1801, King-Harman.
7. KW – her brother Robert, 2 November 1802, King-Harman.
8. KW – her brother Robert, 10 July 1803, King-Harman.
9. KW – her sister Harriet, 21 October 1806, Wilmot MS. RIA.
10. KW – to her sister-in-law Anna Chetwood, 1 October 1805, Wilmot MS. RIA.

1 Travelling Companions

1. Edward C. McAleer, *The Sensitive Plant. A Life of Lady Mount Cashell* (1958), p. 5.
2. *Ibid.*, p. 6.
3. *Ibid.*
4. *Ibid.*, p. 66.
5. *Sadleir*, p. viii.
6. KW – her brother Robert, 24 November 1801, King-Harman.
7. *A Chaplain in Paris 1801–1802*, ed. A. M. Broadley (1913), p. 16.
8. *Ibid.*, p. 60.
9. Edmund John Eyre, *Observations made at Paris during the Peace* (1803), p. 114.
10. *A Chaplain in Paris 1801–1802*, ed. A. M. Broadley (1913), p. 171.
11. *Journal and Correspondence of Miss Berry*, ed. Lady Theresa Lewis (1865), Vol. II, p. 135.
12. *Life and Letters of Maria Edgeworth*, ed. Augustus

179

J. C. Hare (1894), Vol. I, p. 115.

13. John Carr Esq., *The Stranger in France or A Tour from Devonshire to Paris* (1803), p. 103.
14. *Ibid.*, p. 102.
15. *Ibid.*
16. *Journal and Correspondence of Miss Berry*, ed. Lady Theresa Lewis (1865), Vol. II, p. 177.
17. *Ibid.*, p. 177.
18. *The Journals and Letters of Fanny Burney*, ed. Hemlow (1975), p. 269.
19. *Journal and Correspondence of Miss Berry*, ed. Lady Theresa Lewis (1865), Vol. II, p. 164.

2 Continental Journal

29 November – 31 January 1802

1. *Journal and Correspondence of Miss Berry*, ed. Lady Theresa Lewis (1865), Vol. II, p. 181.
2. *Ibid.*, p. 180.
3. *A Chaplain in Paris 1801–1802*, ed. A. M. Broadley (1913), p. 47.
4. *Ibid.*, p. 77.

13 March – 13 October 1802

1. Edward C. McAleer, *The Sensitive Plant. A Life of Lady Mount Cashell* (1958), p. 6.
2. KW – her brother Robert, 30 August 1802, King-Harman.
3. KW – her brother Robert, 6 October 1802, King-Harman.

19 October – 17 December 1802

1. KW – her brother Robert, Milan, 15 November 1802, King-Harman.
2. *Ibid.*

1 January – 6 March 1803

1. KW – her brother Robert, 1 January 1803, King-Harman.
2. *Ibid.*
3. *Ibid.*

17 April – 10 July 1803

1. KW – her brother Robert, 17 April 1803, King-Harman.
2. *Ibid.*
3. *Londonderry*, p. 50.

1 – 19 September 1803

1. Edward C. McAleer, *The Sensitive Plant. A Life of Lady Mount Cashell* (1958), p. 7.
2. *Ibid.*
3. *Ibid.*
4. KW – her brother Robert, 19 July 1803, King-Harman.
5. KW – her brother Robert, Tuesday, 16 August 1803, King-Harman.
6. *Ibid.*
7. KW – her brother, Robert, 23 August 1803, King-Harman.

3 The Visit to the Great Bear

1. *Londonderry*, p. 50.
2. *Memoirs of Princess Dashkov*, ed. Mrs W. Bradford (1840), Vol. II, p. 217.

3. *Ibid.*, p. 218.
4. *Ibid.*, p. 223.
5. *Letters of Horace Walpole*, ed. Toynbee, Vol. VII, p. 420.
6. *Memoirs of Princess Dashkov*, ed. Mrs W. Bradford (1840), Vol. II, p. 225.
7. *Ibid.*
8. *Londonderry*, p. 62.
9. *Ibid.*, p. 68.
10. *Ibid.*, p. 85.
11. *Ibid.*, p. xx.
12. *Ibid.*, p. 143.
13. *Ibid.*, p. 145.
14. Wm. Mavor, *Universal History* (1808), Vol. XXII, p. 1.
15. W. Richardson, *Anecdotes of the Russian Empire* (1783), p. 249.
16. *Ibid.*, p. 194.
17. Elizabeth Lady Craven, *Journey through the Crimea to Constantinople* (1789), p. 141.

4 Russian Journal

4 – 31 August 1805

No notes.

9 September – 8 December 1805

1. KW – her sister-in-law Anna Chetwood, 24 September [1805], Wilmot MS. RIA.
2. *Londonderry*, p. 150.
3. KW – her sister-in-law Anna Chetwood, 24 September [1805], Wilmot MS. RIA.

4. *Londonderry*, p. 154.
5. KW – her sister Alicia, 7 December [1805], unpublished Wilmot MS. RIA.

15 December 1805 – 21 October 1806

1. KW – her sister Alicia, 18 February 1806, unpublished Wilmot MS. RIA.
2. *Londonderry*, p. 267.
3. KW – her sister-in-law Anna Chetwood, Friday 21 March NS 1806, unpublished Wilmot MS. RIA.
4. KW – her sister-in-law, Anna Chetwood, 27 June 1806, unpublished Wilmot MS. RIA.
5. *Londonderry*, p. 268.
6. *Ibid.*, p. 269.
7. *Ibid.*, p. 298.
8. *Ibid.*, p. 271.
9. KW – the Rev John Chetwood, 14 October 1806, Wilmot MS. RIA.
10. *Londonderry*, p. 272.
11. *Ibid.*
12. *Ibid.*

15 November 1806 – 17 September 1807

1. *Londonderry*, p. 273.
2. KW – her sister-in-law Anna Chetwood, 2 February 1807, unpublished Wilmot MS. RIA.
3. *Londonderry*, p. 273.

4. κw's Personal Journal, 28 December 1806, unpublished Wilmot MS. RIA.
5. *Londonderry*, p. 293.
6. *Ibid.*, p. 280.
7. *Ibid.*, p. 285.
8. κw – her sister-in-law Anna Chetwood, 2 February 1807, unpublished Wilmot MS. RIA.
9. κw – her friend Anne Latham, 15 May 1807, Wilmot MS. RIA.
10. *Londonderry*, p. 286.
11. κw – her friend Anne Latham, 15 May 1807, Wilmot MS. RIA.
12. κw's Personal Journal, Monday 23 February [1807], unpublished Wilmot MS. RIA.
13. *Ibid.*, Monday 1 March [1807].
14. *Ibid.*, Monday 15 March [1807].
15. *Ibid.*, Monday 3 May 1807.
16. *Ibid.*, Monday 10 May 1807.
17. *Ibid.*, Monday 14 June [1807].
18. *Ibid.*, Monday 28 June [1807].
19. *Ibid.*, Monday 5 July 1807.
20. *Ibid.*, Monday 12 July [1807].
21. *Ibid.*, Monday 26 July 1807.
22. *Ibid.*, Monday 2 August [1807], at sea.
23. *Ibid.*, Monday 10 [sic] August [1807], at sea.
24. *Ibid.*, Monday 17 August [1807], at sea.
25. *Ibid.*
26. *Ibid.*
27. *Ibid.*
28. *Ibid.*, Monday 31 August [1807], at sea.
29. *Ibid.*, Monday 7 September [1807], off Yarmouth.
30. *Ibid.*, Monday 14 September [1807], London, Osborne's Family Hotel, Adelphi.

Postscript

1. κw's Personal Journal, Bruce Castle, Monday 21 September 1807, unpublished Wilmot MS. RIA.
2. *Londonderry*, p. 309.
3. *Ibid.*, p. 382.
4. *Ibid.*, p. xxiii.
5. *Ibid.*, p. xxv.

Index